Climbing the Academic Ladder:
Doctoral Women Scientists in Academe

A Report to the
Office of Science and Technology Policy

from the
Committee on the Education and Employment
of Women in Science and Engineering

Commission on Human Resources
National Research Council

National Academy of Sciences
Washington, D.C. 1979

NOTICE

The project that is the subject of this report was approved by the Governing Board of the National Research Council, whose members are drawn from the Councils of the National Academy of Sciences, the National Academy of Engineering, and the Institute of Medicine. The members of the Committee responsible for the report were chosen for their special competences and with regard for appropriate balance.

This report has been reviewed by a group other than the authors according to procedures approved by a Report Review Committee consisting of members of the National Academy of Sciences, the National Academy of Engineering, and the Institute of Medicine.

International Standard Book Number 0-309-02880-9

Library of Congress Catalog Card Number 79-87666

Available from

Office of Publications
National Academy of Sciences
2101 Constitution Avenue, N.W.
Washington, D.C. 20418

Printed in the United States of America

Elizabeth L. SCOTT
    Professor of Statistics
    University of California, Berkeley

Robert J. SLATER
    Director of Medical Programs
    National Multiple Sclerosis Society

Members of the Committee who served in earlier formative years
of this report are:

Mildred S. DRESSELHAUS
    Department of Electrical Engineering
    Massachusetts Institute of Technology

Patricia A. GRAHAM
    Radcliffe Institute and Harvard University

Naomi McAFEE
    Systems and Technology Divisions
    Westinghouse Electric Corporation

Jeremiah P. OSTRIKER
    Princeton University Observatory

Janet T. SPENCE
    Department of Psychology
    The University of Texas at Austin

Table of Contents

LIST OF TABLES

LIST OF FIGURES

PREFACE

This report focuses on the status of women scientists in academic institutions, the major employer of doctoral scientists. It also examines their current situation in postdoctoral training and their role in national science advisory bodies, entities that draw their membership primarily from academe. A future report of this Committee will analyze the employment of women scientists and engineers in government and industry.

The Committee on the Education and Employment of Women in Science and Engineering was established by the Commission on Human Resources of the National Research Council in December 1974. Its charge was to analyze the social and institutional constraints that limit the participation of women in science and engineering and to examine the problems of sex discrimination in their education and employment.

Since its inception, the Committee has been chaired by Lilli S. Hornig, Executive Director of Higher Education Resource Services of New England. She has led the Committee through the processes of formulating specific tasks, obtaining funds and staff, and completing their report.

Preparation of the report began in the summer of 1977 when the Committee undertook the task of preparing studies of the education and employment of women scientists and engineers for the Office of Science and Technology Policy (OSTP) in order to illuminate national policy issues in these areas. Since September 15, 1977, the work of the Committee has been conducted pursuant to Task Order No. 365 (OSTP 77-9) of National Science Foundation Contract C310, under OSTP's first contract in the area of human resources. Gilbert S. Omenn, Associate Director for Human Resources and Social and Economic Services, OSTP, has provided technical liaison for this report.

In fulfilling its assignment, the Committee has been primarily concerned with the analysis of the trends of the last few years in the education and employment of women scientists. It has sought to assess the effectiveness of existing remedial practices and to indicate additional measures that would contribute to more balanced faculties and advisory committees.

Data for the report were obtained from surveys of the Commission on Human Resources; the files on advisory committee members of the Alcohol, Drug Abuse, and Mental Health Administration, the National Institutes of Health, the National Research Council, and the National Science Foundation; and published sources.

Acknowledgments

Many scientific organizations and individuals have contributed data, advice, and general support to the Committee and staff during preparation of this report.

The financial support provided by the Office of Science and Technology Policy has been noted above and is most gratefully acknowledged.

Within the National Research Council, the Committee has received guidance, advice, and encouragement from the Commission on Human Resources, especially from Robert A. Alberty and Harrison Shull, successive chairmen of the Commission; and from Albert Clogston, Dorothea Jameson, and Charles Kidd, who served as Commission reviewers for the report.

Members of the staff of the Commission on Human Resources who assisted the Committee in the preparation of this report include Nancy C. Ahern, Staff Officer for the Committee since November, 1978; Leila Rosen Young, who served as Staff Officer from January, 1978 through August, 1978; and Milda H. Vaivada, Administrative Assistant throughout the course of the study. Joan Snyder, serving as consultant, edited the report and contributed to its organization. William C. Kelly, Executive Director of the Commission, provided administrative guidance to the Committee and Staff.

Helpful contributions and encouragement to the work of the Committee have been made by Gilbert S. Omenn, Associate Director for Human Resources and Social and Economic Services, Office of Science and Technology Policy.

To these and many other individuals and organizations who helped, the Committee expresses its sincere thanks.

SUMMARY OF FINDINGS

- The majority of women scientists under discussion in this report received their undergraduate education and were admitted to graduate school well before the advent of equal opportunity mandates in higher education.

- Women scientists receive their graduate education in the same institutions as men but in much smaller numbers. Similar proportions of men and women are trained in the highest-rated departments.

- On the average, as measured by college grades and high school test scores, women scientists at receipt of the doctorate show evidence of higher academic ability than men and, in recent years, have completed their Ph.D.s as fast as or faster than men. This finding supports the inference that women may have been more highly selected. Comparisons of research ability cannot be made unambiguously at this stage since no reliable measures are applicable.

- Of the new Ph.D.s who were seeking postdoctoral appointments, the men were in general more likely to receive early awards.

- The universities ranked highest by R&D expenditures, which have traditionally employed the fewest women, have made the greatest relative gains in appointing new women faculty at all ranks, in spite of the fact that this group of institutions sustained the lowest growth rates in the sciences in recent years.

- Women science faculties increased about three times faster than total faculty growth between 1973 and 1977.

- Science faculties at ladder ranks in all institutions increased by 22,000 between 1973 and 1977; women's share of that increase was 21 percent, somewhat larger than their share of doctorates since 1970. This finding suggests that some women faculty were recruited from among long-term postdoctorals and research staffs.

- Women account for all of the net growth in science faculty at the assistant professor rank in the top 50 universities (by R&D expenditures) and for nearly half of the increase in all other institutions.

- At full professorial rank, women account for 19 percent of the net growth between 1973 and 1977 in the top 50 universities, but only 6 percent in the remaining institutions. The respective percentages for associate professors are 69 and 16 percent.

- For all science and engineering fields combined, women's share of faculty appointments (excluding instructor/lecturer) grew from 12 to 19 percent in the second 25 institutions, and from 12 to 18 percent in all others between 1973 and 1977.

- Women's distribution among faculty ranks is a mirror image of men's; women are most likely to be assistant professors but men are most likely to be full professors. In the top 25 institutions, women are more than seven times more likely than men to be at the rank of instructor/lecturer; in 1977 they held 46 percent of these positions compared to 27 percent in 1973.

- Rank for rank, women faculty continued to be tenured less often than men; for all ranks, 72 percent of the men but only 46 percent of the women hold tenure appointments. This disparity is increasing.

- Sex differences in salaries remains a serious problem. Median salary differentials between women and men in 1977 varied by fields, ranging as high as 28 percent for full professors of chemistry.

- In relation to the pools of new women Ph.D.s in the various fields, chemistry and mathematics employ far lower proportions of women faculty than do other fields.

- Wide field variations in rank, salary, and tenure distribution for women faculty compared to men suggest that an assumed lack of mobility of married women is at most a contributory rather than a primary reason for women's evident disadvantage.

- Research productivity cannot be used yet as an overall comparative measure of male and female academic scientists' performance. In most fields in research universities, there are not yet enough women faculty who have held professional positions with the necessary perquisites long enough to make such comparisons meaningful.

- The Alcohol, Drug Abuse, and Mental Health Administration, the National Institutes of Health, and the National Science Foundation have shown marked gains in the percentages of women appointed to advisory committees,

while the National Research Council has not yet matched
the representation of women in the appropriate doctoral
pool.

- In the past few years women have been 6 to 8 percent of
  newly elected NAS members, more than twice their share of
  full professorships in high-ranking research universities.

- The number of women scientists in tenure-track positions
  in research universities and in policy advisory
  functions is slowly increasing as a result of affirmative
  action. Sex differences in salaries and awarding of
  tenure persist.

INTRODUCTION

Overview

Why are there so few women scientists? Why do we so rarely hear of their work? What happens to the over two thousand women who annually earn doctorates in science? What jobs do they get? _Do_ they get jobs? Dead end jobs, or those with a future? Do they get equal pay for equal work? Have equal opportunity mandates changed their situation? Do they benefit as men do from public awareness of their work? Do they have similar opportunities to serve in policy advisory bodies? What is the outlook for their future?

We chose to focus this first report on academic employment, primarily in faculty positions, both because existing data are more extensive than for other sectors and because educational institutions are the prime employers of doctoral scientists. In addition, the hierarchy of ranks and institutions is well-defined and makes it possible to compare how men and women fare in professional terms to a degree that is not readily matched in industry, for example. Beyond these pragmatic considerations, however, faculty status represents the quintessential scientific career. Ideally it provides total freedom of inquiry, insured by a degree of personal security unmatched in any other walk of life except the Civil Service. In practice, freedom of inquiry may be somewhat curbed by the availability of money and more recently by certain external regulations. Still, to many young scientists a tenured faculty post in a research university remains the most desirable career goal. How many women reach it?

Scientific manpower has been the subject of many analyses since World War II; scientific womanpower--about one-tenth of the scientific doctoral labor force--has received little attention until recently, when equal opportunity legislation required employers to perform utilization analyses of their labor force. Data on doctorate production by sex and field have been published since 1920, but detailed employment information on a national sample of all science and engineering Ph.D's has been available only since 1973. While some analyses of women scientists' employment for individual disciplines have

1

appeared in the last few years, no systematic studies encompassing all science fields have been done.

This Committee owes its existence to the pressures arising from the women's movement, specifically in academe, during the late sixties. A small conference was convened by the National Academy of Sciences in 1972 to begin exploration of women's status in science, followed by a research conference in 1974. Subsequently, this Committee was appointed. Concurrently, demands from employers, particularly academic institutions, for better information regarding women scientists arose in relation to their affirmative action obligations.

Scope of the Study

To assess whether and to what extent earlier patterns of faculty appointments have changed since the advent of affirmative action regulations, we will be examining extensive trend data on the production and employment of men and women doctorates. We hoped that it would be possible also to derive some insights that transcend statistical comparisons. The flow of scientists through graduate and postdoctoral training and into jobs, in academe or elsewhere, is subject to various influences not usually considered in affirmative action discussions. Training opportunities at both pre- and postdoctoral levels are highly dependent on research funding, which has been changing in the last decade, declining in real dollars and fluctuating widely among fields. The effects of the Vietnam War and the draft on science doctorates are almost impossible to assess. To what extent, if at all, did they reduce the numbers of new male doctorates or affect their quality? We have no data on this and can draw no conclusions. The decreasing enrollments in higher education are reducing the number of available appointments; some departments are contracting, and almost all are postponing tenure decisions as long as possible. Against such a background, what kind of hiring and promotion rates for women scientists can reasonably be expected? How do we interpret the changes we find? If no expansion is possible, what might the "good will efforts" which the law is willing to accept in lieu of actual numerical improvement encompass?

What of the problems of obsolescence which are specific to science and not to other academic disciplines? A first-rate woman scientist trained a decade ago and unlikely to be considered at that time for a faculty post in a research university may have spent the intervening years teaching in a small college. Her ten-year-old qualifications do not fit her now for the position she should have had then. Can anything be done for her? Should something be done? Could her excellent capabilities, maturity, and experience in a

2

different sector of academic science be used to advantage in advisory functions? How many others like her are there? Is this a national problem?

What are the restrictions faced by women who decide to interrupt or slow down their careers in order to have children? Are there employment options available that would utilize their talent on a rigorous but less than full-time basis? There is a continuing search by today's young men and women for ways to reconcile conflicting demands of their parental and career roles. While academic institutions cannot be charged with responsibility for either the problems or solutions that women face in this connection, they should avoid compounding the problem and should share responsiblity for exploring the development of solutions within the academic framework that would help meet the conflicts. For example, a quarter of a century ago New York Medical College took the pioneering step of offering part-time psychiatric residency for women physicians with young families.

We have also been mindful of the compounded difficulties faced by minority women scientists; their problems are discussed fully in a conference report issued by the American Association for the Advancement of Science (1977). It is interesting to note here that minority women report more discrimination based on sex than on race. For the purposes of this report, we found minority women scientists to be too widely scattered through fields and departments to enable us to draw any general conclusions other than to deplore their absence.

At the end of this report we consider the possible modifications or policy initiatives which could correct or ameliorate existing inequities. Among these are the creation of additional research opportunities, more innovative institutional contributions to solving dual-career problems, and expanded opportunites for service by women scientists in advisory functions. It is notoriously difficult, however, to devise remedial policies which do not in turn create some measure of disadvantage for innocent bystanders.

Implicit in these questions is our assumption that men and women scientists are of comparable quality. Some scientists do not believe that assumption is justified, Lester (1974) among them. We explore that problem in Chapter 2, insofar as the usual proxy measures of ability can be applied. None of them really tells us much about research potential, or how we foretell the excellent from the merely very good.

It is often assumed that women's careers must necessarily take a different path from men's because of their different family responsibilities and constraints on mobility. If that is true, and given similar ratios of qualified candidates, unmarried women's career opportunities should be just like men's, and there should be no systematic differences in relative employment of women among fields unless some fields somehow impose greater demands on their practitioners than do others.

As we begin this exploration, it must be stressed again that our concern is with the status of women scientists, rather than the situation of all women doctorates. Excellence in science, at least at advanced levels, can be fostered only in certain circumstances. It is far more dependent than other fields on concentrations of facilities and equipment and the presence of other workers in the same or related disciplines. The place where a potentially outstanding scientist finds employment, and the conditions of such employment, will therefore influence the eventual realization of that potential in significant ways.

On the other hand, science demands aptitudes and preparation possibly more specialized or exacting than other disciplines so that we must examine the capacities of men and women scientists as they enter their professional careers. For this purpose, a comparison of all women doctorates with all men doctorates is inappropriate. Numerous comparisons of this type have yielded negative results for women with respect to measures of educational quality. In fact, these distinctions reflect the different field distributions of the two sexes. The fact that women doctorates as a group take longer than men to complete their degrees, for example, simply indexes the greater concentration of women in nonscience fields where both sexes customarily obtain their degrees after longer time periods.

Our analysis, therefore, is limited to a comparison of men and women Ph.D.'s in the natural sciences, the social sciences, and engineering. It excludes those with doctorates in other fields as well as those with professional degrees in fields such as medicine but does include Ph.D.'s employed in medical or other professional schools.

EQUAL OPPORTUNITY IN HIGHER EDUCATION

In 1968, Executive Order 11246 extended the clause of the 1964 Civil Rights Act prohibiting discrimination in employment (Title VII) to cover institutions of higher education, which were previously excluded, and four years later the Office of Civil Rights issued its Guidelines for Affirmative Action in Higher Education to implement Title VII. Also in 1972, Title IX of the Higher Education Amendments specifically addressed the provision for

4

educational equity at all levels. Equal opportunity for study and employment in higher education regardless of sex is therefore a clearly stated goal of national policy; the explicit controversies surrounding the issue have dealt not with the desirability of achieving that equality but with the means for doing so. Since affirmative action guidelines require utilization analyses based on appropriate statistical information, there has been a natural tendency, for purposes of both general discussion and the establishment of legal evidence, to argue for or against the existence of discrimination on statistical grounds. Any discrepancy between the percentage of women or minorities qualified by training and experience to hold a given type of position and the percentage actually employed has been taken as legal evidence of discrimination, purposeful or not. (Relevant legislation and Executive Orders are summarized in Appendix A.)

Several assumptions and issues are buried in the foregoing paragraph. The fact that equal opportunity laws came into being strongly suggests that equal opportunity had not existed previously. Was this a valid assumption? We think so. Until a decade ago, women were not admitted as undergraduates, and in some cases not as graduate students, to several highly selective universities which set the pace for academic science. Women who were admitted to graduate and professional schools sometimes had to meet higher standards. Numerous instances of more stringent criteria for the admission of women to selective graduate departments were cited by Harris (Harris, 1970). An illustrative case is that of the School of Veterinary Science, University of Pennsylvania, which until recently required a 3.6 GPA of women applicants and 2.6 of men (Davies, 1978).

Major universities rarely appointed women to their science faculties (although the pool of pre-1950 Ph.D.'s included about ten percent women). Women were more likely to be employed by colleges and non-research universities and to be concentrated in the lower ranks or as research staff. Moreover, they were not paid as much as similarly trained men at the same rank. For example, in 1973, a woman full professor was typically paid 15 to 20 percent less than a man in three major fields--chemistry, biology, and social sciences.[1]

Was all this a result of discrimination? Some spokesmen for the universities have argued otherwise, suggesting that women preferred less demanding occupations in order to fulfill their family obligations, that restricted mobility made a normal academic career almost impossible for them, and that they were paid all they were worth. (See Lester, 1974, for an extended exposition of this point of view.)

These arguments in turn rest on assumptions about the nature of academic careers and the relative abilities of women and men, and the likely responses of the two groups to potential conflicts between professional demands and family obligations. The commitment in time, energy, and dedication required of a tenured faculty member is large, and may in fact conflict with many other desired activities for men as well as women. The degree of flexibility a tenured appointment permits is also very high, however, and this might be more important in accommodating other obligations than the high total level of effort. In any case, these considerations are speculative; very little is known about how scientists make career choices at this level, or how they assess personal costs against potential professional benefits. Instances of either male or female scientists refusing academic appointments solely because they are too demanding appear to be rare at best. The inference that women commonly do so while men do not is unsupported.

Restrictions on geographic mobility for career development pose a different sort of problem. Under present social circumstances, most women with families are probably in fact less mobile than men, although "commuter couples" are increasingly common in academe. A parallel flexibility on the part of universities in creating joint employment for such couples exists in a few cases but is not widespread. In any case we know little about the professional benefits-- or costs--of high mobility, or indeed about its incidence among scientists. A year or two devoted to rebuilding a research group and reorganizing facilities following a professional move may represent a long-term loss of research productivity which actually overshadows the gains in professional opportunity or other benefits. Whether women faculty members are less likely than men to move for better opportunity, or whether they are less likely to have the opportunity to move, remain unresolved questions.

Legal Definitions

Regardless of the basis for limitations on the status of women in academe, equal opportunity laws do not distinguish intent from historical accident; they deal only with end results. If women or other "affected groups" appear in a given employee category in proportions lower than their representation in the appropriate availability pool they are assumed to be victims of discrimination in the first instance. At this writing, the burden of proving otherwise legally rests with the employer.

Affirmative action policies, their execution, and the controversy surrounding them deserve futher comment here. As the regulations apply to faculty employment, they require equal opportunity to be considered for a job and selection

6

on merit criteria only, with the choice between two equally matched candidates to favor a woman or minority candidate. To ascertain whether their choices are indeed bias free, institutions are required to perform periodic utilization analyses and set goals and timetables for rectifying imbalances. However, relatively few universities have affirmative action plans which actually contain numerical goals, and they have enjoyed considerable latitude in setting those goals on the basis of their own internal staffing projections. More important, the penalties provided by law--the withholding of federal monies until an institution is in compliance--have only been imposed on a token basis, i.e., for a period of a week or two until the institution agreed to come into compliance at some future time. The most important sanction which the law provides is a pre-award compliance review conducted on site for grants and contracts exceeding $1 million; after six years, it was applied for the first time in the last few months. At this writing, most of these reviews are incomplete and it is too early to judge their general effect.

Any conclusions regarding the effectiveness of affirmative action policies unfortunately will be clouded by the widely acknowledged capriciousness of enforcement efforts, the sometimes highly localized interpretations of regulations by enforcement officers, and the frequent problems which have been generated by these actions.

Unresolved Issues

The questions we have posed, and addressed throughout this report, deal with the opportunities afforded to individual women scientists (although they must be framed in terms of groups of individuals). Another set of issues concerns the universities and the fabric of science itself. Can it be argued that the major universities have impoverished themselves by virtually excluding women from their faculties? Are science departments of lower quality than they would be had they hired more women? Will they be better if and when they do? Would there be more women science students if there were more women science faculty? Would that provide a welcome source of additional talent, or merely flood already overpopulated fields?

Answers to such questions would remain speculative at best, and none are suggested, but readers should bear these issues in mind.

Data Sources

The tools at our disposal for examining these issues are the extensive and detailed data collected by the National

7

Research Council in its Surveys of Earned Doctorates and
Comprehensive Surveys of Doctorate Recipients.[2] These are
the only available longitudinal data that encompass Ph.D.'s
in all science and engineering fields.

The Survey of Earned Doctorates, an annual survey
containing responses of virtually all new Ph.D.'s in the
United States, provides data on background characteristics,
educational patterns, and post-degree plans at the time the
degree is obtained. The present report relies heavily on
this source for data on the 1977 doctorates and, for
information on earlier cohorts, on the accumulated data from
these surveys, referred to as the Doctorate Records File.
In some instances, tabulations of these data by field and
sex reveal very few cases in specific cells, e.g., women in
physical sciences, but it should be stressed that these
numbers reflect the entire population, rather than a sample,
of the Ph.D's in a given category. Sampling error is not a
consideration with respect to these tables (Tables 2.1, 2.4-
2.7, 2.10-3.2, and 3.5).

In contrast, the biennial Survey of Doctorate Recipients
is administered to a sample. The sample of 65,000 doctoral
scientists and enginers is drawn primarily from the
Doctorate Records File but also includes some individuals
who earned their doctorates at foreign institutions. Data
in this report on employment status, sector, activity, rank,
and salary are from this source. The numbers in the tables
from the Survey of Doctorate Recipients represent the sample
weighted to yield an estimate of the doctoral population in
the national labor force.

In addition to these two major sources of statistical
data, numerous individual studies and reports have been
reviewed, and reference is made to these throughout the
report.

Limitations of the Data

In tabulations from the Survey of Doctorate Recipients,
small estimates may reflect even smaller numbers of sample
cases. When the number of sample individuals in a cell is
fewer than three, no figures or percentages are presented.
For other cells containing small numbers for the estimated
population, the reader is urged to exercise great caution in
the interpretation of percentages. This reminder is
repeated in a footnote on each table from the Survey of
Doctorate Recipients (Tables 2.8, 2.9, 3.3, 3.4, and 3.6-
4.20). A discussion of the survey is included in Appendix
D.

On other grounds, statistical findings must be applied
with caution to determinations of sex discrimination; group

differences in quality or mobility would produce entirely legitimate statistical biases, for example. In addition, each academic hiring decision is in some sense unique and will involve personal assessments which, no matter how sincerely performed, may be swayed by one prejudice or another. In the absence of systematic sex discrimination in academic appointments, however, the sum of such individual decisions as reflected in aggregate statistics should not show bias but reflect the sex distribution of the available scientists of comparable quality.

A further limitation in examining statistical data, however disaggregated, is that they cannot tell us much about the flow of individuals through the various professional levels. For example, we cannot tell whether the increase seen in numbers of women at senior ranks in some fields represents an upgrading of in-house candidates or recruitment from other institutions. Nor do the data allow us to distinguish between those junior research faculty members who move up and those who are forced to move out.

Organization of the Report

The first chapter of the report examines some of the obstacles that women must overcome to become professional scientists. The following chapter assesses the characteristics, educational patterns, and supply of women doctorates in the sciences. Chapter 3 examines sex differences in postdoctoral training patterns. The fourth chapter presents recent developments in the academic employment of men and women scientists. Chapter 5 reviews the participation of women in three major groups within the national science advisory apparatus. The sixth chapter provides an overview of the current prospects of women scientists in academe as well as recommendations for improving these prospects.

NOTES

1   See Table 4.19A on page 90.

2   These are described in Appendix C and D, respectively, and copies of the questionnaires are included.

CHAPTER 1

CONSTRAINTS, BARRIERS AND POTENTIAL

The evidence in this report shows, as have previous studies, that women are represented in very small percentages in the doctoral labor force of engineering and the physical sciences. The percentages are somewhat larger in the life sciences, psychology, and the social sciences, but even in psychology, the major field with the largest participation by women, women were only 23 percent of the doctoral labor force in 1977 (Table 2.8).

Not only are there relatively few women scientists and engineers in the labor force, but employed women scientists have not shared their men colleagues' advancement in either position or salary. Two general questions emerge from this picture: why are there so few women scientists, and why is their progress so slow? To approach these questions it is appropriate to consider, albeit briefly, some of the constraints and barriers that have contributed to the paucity of women among the ranks of professional scientists and engineers.

Sex Differences in Scientific Aptitude

There are certain widely held ideas concerning areas of sex differences, and in the past it has been difficult--for specialists as well as for nonspecialists--to assess the validity of these ideas due to inadequate knowledge or research about human behavior. There is now an encyclopedic compilation and discussion of the results of psychological research on sex differences by Maccoby and Jacklin (1974), which makes possible a clearer understanding of what is myth, what is fact, and what has not yet been established. It should be noted that Maccoby and Jacklin find very few documentable differences between the sexes, and that the large majority of studies they review has focused on children.

The data presented and carefully analyzed by these psychologists include some that are especially pertinent to this report. It has been shown, for example, that the two sexes are similar in their early acquisition of quantitative

11

concepts and their mastery of arithmetic in grade school, but that boys' mathematical skills increase faster than girls' from about age 12. The solving of mathematical problems requires, in varying degrees, verbal skills at which more girls than boys excel (Maccoby and Jacklin, 1974, pp. 75 ff.), visual-spatial ability at which more boys than girls excel (pp. 89 ff.), and analytical capacities in which there are no sex differences (pp. 98 ff.). Thus, it is not certain how much of the sex difference in observed mathematical ability results from the difference in visual-spatial ability, and how much can be accounted for on the basis of exposure to and encouragement in mathematics during secondary school and thereafter. However, even if it were found that more boys than girls were genetically endowed to be facile in mathematics, there are obviously other factors that contribute to the 14-fold difference in the number of women and men who have received science doctorates.

One broad consideration relates to the fact that, at all levels of schooling, until recently fewer girls than boys have proceeded to the next level even though, at each level, girls have regularly received higher grades.[1] This attrition of girls and young women from the educational ladder has had an effect on all areas of endeavor, including the pool of doctoral scientists. Can the less frequent participation of females through the ranks of formal education be accounted for on the basis of motivation?

The design of research in this area is such that we have clues only to some elements of the larger dynamic of achievement motivation. Both girls and boys demonstrate motivation to achieve (Maccoby and Jacklin, 1974, pp. 135 ff.), and the few sex differences that are observable when success is measured by some objective standard, such as school performance through the high school years, show superior achievement by girls (pp. 135-136). There is some evidence to suggest that boys' achievement motivation is stimulated by competitive conditions, that is, by the prospect of being compared favorably with respect to peers. Girls appear better able to sustain motivation for achievement in the absence of such conditions (pp. 141, 149).

Closely related to achievement motivation are self-esteem and self-confidence. When females and males rate themselves in these areas (in the absence of comparisons with others), the results are strikingly similar (Maccoby and Jacklin, pp. 150-153). However, in spite of these attitudinal similarities, males approach a variety of tasks, particularly new ones, with more confidence than do females. Although women apply high standards to their work and perform well, they predict that they will not do as well in the future as their previous performance would indicate (p. 154). By the time of the college years, women believe that

12

their achievements are due to factors other than their own skills and hard work. In contrast, men exhibit a marked sense of personal potency: they believe they have the power to control their own destiny, they overestimate their position in the dominance hierarchy, and their sense of self-worth is enhanced by positive feedback while they are relatively insensitive to (do not seem to "hear") negative feedback (pp. 157-158).

The sex differences addressed here, namely the verbal and visual-spatial differences that emerge at about age 12, and the differences in perceived sense of personal potency and interpersonal competitiveness that emerge at about age 17 or 18, appear to be the ones most relevant to an aptitude for science. However, there is a lack of data to indicate the extent to which these aptitudes or behaviors are essential for individuals entering scientific careers. The remainder of this chapter, based on a number of retrospective studies (see, for example, NRC 1975a, and references cited therein), will discuss the personal qualities, motives, educational opportunities, and categories of significant others that, together, seem to have influenced individuals in becoming scientists.

Cultural and Structural Barriers

It is unnecessary to provide documentation that science and technology have been considered--until recent times--inappropriate careers for women in our society, so ubiquitous has been this belief. In this section we shall examine briefly some of the cultural and structural barriers encountered by girls and women in acquiring their formal education.

As we noted earlier, the differences in the skills of boys and girls, which are minimal or nonexistent during the primary school years, begin to appear at adolescence. The factors that assume importance at this time and ultimately produce distinct educational outcomes for men and women require investigation. Traditionally, this was the time at which training diverged--boys could take mechanical drawing while girls could not. Less obvious developments may also produce significant results. In a study conducted some time ago, the values of peer groups in coeducational high schools were shown to be related to the limitation of girls' aspirations and performance (Coleman, 1961). We need to know whether such values have been altered in a new social climate and what other influences are significant as adolescents begin to plan for their adult roles.

In any event, at the secondary school level, the percentage of girls participating in mathematics and science courses decreases as the sophistication of these courses increases, dropping sharply when the courses are not required (Ernest, 1976). The decreases in participation are so large that we may surmise a lack of encouragement or expectation is a factor.

In turn, preparation that has been marginal or inadequate in high school predisposes to low participation by women in science and mathematics courses during the college years. Thus the size of the pool of women with appropriate credentials for continuing to graduate science programs is considerably smaller than would be expected solely on the basis of academic ability and the range of courses available in secondary school and college. Indeed, measured by ratings at the secondary school level and undergraduate grades (see Chapter 2), women who completed doctorates were, in the aggregate, more highly qualified academically than the men who did so. What happened to the women who were as well qualified as the men?

Studies on undergraduate academic environments have brought to light a number of elements that appear to be closely related to the development of talent in women. Among those most frequently hypothesized is the presence of substantial numbers of women faculty who serve as role models: a strong, positive correlation exists between the proportion of women faculty and the number of women students who are subsequently cited for career achievement (Tidball, 1973). More specifically, the women's colleges, where for many years at least half of the faculty members have been female, have graduated almost one-third of the women who have gone on to receive doctorates in science and engineering, even though these colleges granted less than 15 percent of all bachelor's degrees received by women during the comparable time span (Tidball, 1975). It must be recognized that other factors that exist in the women's colleges may be contributing to such results--distinctive distributions of fields in which degrees are granted, the values that are shared by predominantly female student bodies, and the degree of insulation from male students displaying greater self-confidence. We need to know more about the ways in which these factors operate. It should also be noted that the women's colleges represented by these women achievers and scientists exhibit considerable diversity in terms of admissions selectivity, academic expenditures, geographical location and nature of sponsorship (i.e., private or public).

Women students who subsequently completed doctorates were most likely to have earned BA's, if not from women's colleges, then from baccalaureate institutions that had a long and continuous history of women graduates who attained doctorates, and that offered strong academic preparation in several areas of study (Tidball and Kistiakowsky, 1976).

Aside from the proportion of women faculty, other variables are of considerable significance to the development of talent in women undergraduate students. One of these relates to the attitudes of women and men faculty toward the students they teach and toward themselves as academic professionals. Both women and men faculty tend to be supportive to students of the same sex to a greater extent than those of the opposite sex, and far more women than men are in tune with issues of particular concern to women in academe (Tidball, 1976). The relatively small proportion of women faculty on most campuses suggests that there will be fewer faculty who believe in women students' competence and hold high expectations for their accomplishment. Additionally, women faculty generally rate themselves as unsuccessful, particularly when they compare themselves with male peers. Elements of professional activity that correlate most strongly with self-assessments of success differ for women and men faculty: women emphasize a variety of elements that includes teaching, alliance with women-related issues, and association with successful men; men exhibit a strong positive focus on the research image of the institution and a strong negative emphasis on teaching (Tidball, 1976). Thus, students are taught by women faculty who tend not to think well of themselves and men faculty who tend to be most supportive of men students but who often do not think well of teaching. The examples of women achievers for students in most undergraduate institutions are faculty clustered in the lower ranks without tenure and faculty whose salaries are lower than those of their male colleagues at every rank. Additionally, women faculty members tend to be underemployed or misemployed so that their energies are dissipated in peripheral activities which do not accord them the professional recognition conferred on male faculty (Reagan and Maynard, 1974).

Career options for science majors have traditionally emphasized the necessity for a full-time commitment, based in part on the relatively high cost of teaching science and hence the investment that has already been made by the time of college graduation. The idea of not "wasting" one's education is applied more vigorously to the science student than to the English major. It is not easy to participate in some scientific endeavor alone, at home, or without benefit of special equipment or facilities. It is also deemed more difficult to keep up in the sciences on a part-time basis or an interrupted schedule. Just how essential full-time and uninterrupted commitment is for those who would contribute to the scientific endeavor has not been put to rigorous test.

If the constraints within the formal setting of undergraduate institutions are compounded by the cultural bias that holds the study of science to be unsuitable for

15

women, it is perhaps not surprising that there are relatively few women scientists.

Graduate education itself is not without additional hurdles for women. The barriers of cultural and structural origin found in the undergraduate setting are intensified, while new constraints appear as the woman comes closer to membership in the profession. Two collections of articles draw attention to many of these constraints: Graduate and Professional Education of Women (American Association of University Women, 1974) and Research Issues in the Employment of Women (NRC, 1975a).

A paper in the latter collection describes the usual situation for women graduate students in science. In Perrucci's study (1975), the graduate students and faculty of six science departments were survey respondents. The results indicate that occupational role socialization in academic science departments may differ for women and men graduate students. Women Ph.D. candidates are more likely than their male classmates to believe that faculty members expect most career goals to be held mainly by men. The extent to which the faculty members of a department do, in fact, attribute these goals primarily to male students is inversely related to the strength of career commitment among women graduate students in that department. Among the departments studied, chemistry had the largest percent of faculty holding such "male-oriented" views (Perrucci, 1975, pp. 109-110).

Questions on attitudes toward female graduate students were also included in the Carnegie Commission's national survey of faculty and graduate students (Feldman, 1974). Male students and faculty agreed, to a greater extent than female students and faculty, that female students are not as dedicated as their male counterparts, although in no case did the proportion in agreement reach 50 percent. In general, agreement was highest in fields with fewer women graduate students. In the sciences, the highest percentages of faculty affirming the lesser dedication of women were found in biochemistry and chemistry with the lowest percentages in anthropology and political science. The greatest student agreement was found in chemistry and botany and the least in psychology (Feldman, 1974, pp. 70-71).

The same study included a more detailed analysis of commitment among men and women students in five science fields having large proportions of respondents agreeing with the lesser dedication of women. In all five fields, the women had higher undergraduate grade point averages than the men. Nevertheless, the female students were more likely than the males to state that inability or emotional strain might lead them to drop out of graduate school. Among students having a close working relationship with a professor, however, women were no more likely than men to anticipate dropping out. Lower percentages of women than men considered their relationships with their closest professors to be of this kind (Feldman, 1974, pp. 112-113).

The assumption that science is a masculine endeavor emerges and re-emerges throughout all phases of women scientists' academic and professional development. The impact of family life--marriage itself as well as the rearing of children--is regularly raised as an issue of major proportions which women are supposed to defend or deny. The conflicts for women between attitudes deemed appropriate for scientific careers and those associated with feminine roles are very real even though the inevitability of such conflicts has not been demonstrated. On the other hand, the practical support structures that would enable women to engage more freely in their work are not regularly and dependably available.

Discrimination against women, as students and as professional scientists, has been well documented. Reference to some of this evidence is presented in other chapters of this report. Anti-nepotism practices in many employment situations, as well as numerous "non-actionable" behaviors, tend to have larger negative effects on women than on men even though they are not strictly illegal or easy to document. Rowe (1974) has constructed an extensive catalog of discriminatory behaviors that regularly impinge upon women and thereby reduce the energies they have available for productive work.

Conclusions

The thrust of this chapter has been to suggest that there are both cultural and structural factors favoring the attrition of girls and women from science programs, starting at an early age. The effects of these factors are cumulative so relatively few of the women who early in life showed an interest and aptitude for science are finally represented among the ranks of professional scientists.

Significant changes in this traditional picture began in the 1960's. The women's movement gave impetus to an immense and highly diverse research endeavor in which scholars from many fields and points of view have addressed issues pertinent to the education and employment of women, including those of women in science and engineering. As this report will show, more women are proceeding from high school to college and on through graduate programs, and more women are seeking and gaining professional employment. The talent pool of women scientists is larger than many have presumed.

Study Recommendations

1.   Research is needed to clarify factors influencing the growing disparity during adolescence between boys' and girls' interest and achievement in mathematics and science.

2.   The marked difference between single-sex and coeducational colleges in focussing women's interests in the sciences suggests the need for closer study of the influence of higher education environments on sex differences.

NOTE

1   A slightly larger percentage of women than men has been enrolling in college since 1972 (NCES,1978, pp. 116-117) but the statements made are relevant for the doctoral population being considered in this report.

CHAPTER 2

THE SUPPLY OF WOMEN DOCTORATES

An assessment of the supply of women doctorates in the various fields of science is essential to an understanding of the career paths of women scientists and an analysis of their relative opportunities. It has long been evident that women constitute small fractions of those earning science doctorates though their numbers vary greatly by field (Table 2.1). Some of the factors associated with this have been indicated in Chapter 1.

The proportion of women doctorates in science compared with the baccalaureate pool is actually much lower than has been recognized so far. The fact that the percentages of science doctorates granted to women have approached or exceeded the levels of the 1920's in the last few years has been widely regarded as a sign of considerable progress (Table 2.1); indeed it is much better than the dismal record just after World War II. However, the levels of the 1920-1929 decade must be compared with the relative supply of baccalaureates then and now; during the earlier period only about half as many women as men completed college, while today their numbers are about equal. The ratio of women doctorates to women baccalaureates is still dramatically smaller than it used to be. Examination of the ratios for men and women in recent years (Table 2.2) shows that the proportion of women B.A.'s who complete Ph.D.'s is still less than half the proportion of men. Nevertheless, while the ratios have steadily declined for both sexes over the last five years, the ratio for men has declined at a much faster rate.

The very low rate of participation in graduate study by women following World War II is largely a result of well-documented overt sex discrimination practiced for many years in some graduate science departments (see, for example, the essays by Evelyn Fox Keller and Naomi Weisstein in Working it Out). Conversely, the high growth rate since the late 1960's of women doctorates in science can be ascribed in large measure to the exposure and consequent easing of overt bias even before 1972, as well as to general changes in the social climate.

TABLE 2.1 Number and Percent of Science and Engineering Doctorates Granted to Women By Field and Decade, 1920-1977

	1920-1929		1930-1939		1940-1949		1950-1959		1960-1969		1970-1977		1920-1977 Total	
	No.	%	No.	%	No.	%	No.	%	No.	%	No.	%	No.	%
All Fields	952	12.2	1,775	11.0	1,731	8.9	3,533	6.7	8,336	12.6	20,554	13.5	36,881	10.4
Physical Sciences	247	7.6	442	6.6	406	5.0	685	3.7	1,577	4.6	3,048	7.4	6,405	5.7
Mathematics	51	14.5	115	14.8	89	10.7	113	5.0	364	5.7	853	9.2	1,585	8.0
Physics/Astron.	39	5.9	51	3.8	62	4.2	98	2.0	213	2.2	449	3.9	912	3.1
Chemistry	141	7.3	254	6.4	223	4.2	443	4.4	931	6.4	1,479	9.8	3,471	6.8
Earth Sciences	16	4.8	22	3.5	32	5.7	31	1.9	69	2.0	267	5.5	437	3.8
Engineering	2	.9	6	.7	7	.5	20	.3	77	.4	311	1.2	423	0.8
Life Sciences	378	15.9	765	15.1	738	12.7	1,318	9.1	3,078	11.6	6,635	17.0	12,912	13.9
Biological	341	19.5	698	17.8	699	15.7	1,174	11.8	2,739	15.1	5,376	20.6	11,027	17.1
Agricultural	8	2.2	11	1.6	5	.6	36	1.1	80	1.4	333	4.2	473	2.5
Medical	29	10.9	56	12.4	34	6.9	108	8.1	259	9.5	926	19.1	1,412	13.9
Social Sciences	325	17.1	562	15.8	580	14.5	1,510	11.0	3,604	14.3	10,560	22.5	17,141	18.0
Anthropology	8	22.2	28	22.4	22	15.2	90	19.3	218	21.5	847	32.4	1,213	27.5
Sociology	32	15.4	89	19.9	99	17.2	221	14.2	442	17.5	1,355	26.5	2,238	21.4
Economics	52	8.5	71	6.4	83	7.1	125	4.2	245	4.6	540	8.0	1,116	6.2
Political Science/ Pub. Adm.	26	9.0	45	8.5	45	7.8	87	5.4	257	8.2	809	13.8	1,269	10.6
Psychology	189	29.4	290	26.0	302	24.1	911	14.8	2,264	20.7	5,995	30.1	9,951	24.8

Source: Doctorate Records File, National Research Council

Table 2.2   Ratio of Ph.D.s Granted in Science and Engineering
in 1973-1977 to B.A.'s Earned 7 Years Earlier, by Sex

	Year of Doctorate				
	1973	1974	1975	1976	1977
Men					
No. Ph.D.'s / No. B.A.'s 7 yrs earlier	10.23%	9.14%	8.11%	6.92%	6.14%
Women					
No. Ph.D.'s / No. B.A.'s 7 yrs earlier	3.69%	3.56%	3.34%	3.00%	2.85%

Source: Data on Ph.D.'s in science and engineering are from the Survey of
Earned Doctorates, National Research Council. Data on baccalaureates
in science and engineering are from the series of reports,
Earned Degrees Conferred, 1965-66 to 1969-70, National Center for
Education Statistics.

Figure 2.1   Ratio of Ph.D.'s Granted in Science
and Engineering in 1973-1977 to BA's
Earned 7 Years Earlier, by Sex

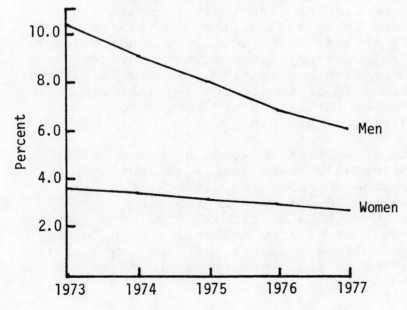

A 1972 study found the ratio of graduate school acceptances to applications to be slightly greater for women than for men (Solmon, 1976, p. 43). It has been pointed out, however, that in some cases, basing admissions on the number of applications of each sex still produced acceptance of poorer male students while better women candidates were rejected (Cross, 1973, p. 41). Since the women applicants must therefore have been a better pool, this result suggests that they may have different perceptions of the standards for viable candidacy. At present we lack the data to tell us how such self-selection operates--the degree to which it is a relatively independent decision of the potential applicant, though reflecting earlier educational experience, and the extent to which it is mediated through advisers and others.

A question of particular interest is whether significant changes took place in the graduate admissions patterns and practices of the distinguished universities whose undergraduate bodies were either exclusively or predominantly male before 1968. Similarly, the graduate education patterns of the new alumnae from these institutions should be followed closely; it is possible that they differ significantly from those of the past, when women had no general access to these undergraduate training opportunities. If that proved to be so, it would suggest accelerating the currently slow movement toward equal access to these universities.

Another issue of importance in graduate training is equality of access to financial support. Aid in the form of fellowships appears to be comparable in amount for men and women but somewhat different in kind, with men more likely to receive research assistantships and women teaching fellowships (Survey of Earned Doctorates, 1977). Such a difference may have far-reaching effects in establishing patterns of interest and in actual quality of graduate training, and requires further investigation. Student loans were less accessible to women until the advent of recent state and Federal legislation prohibiting sex discrimination in credit. The relationship of the recent availability of loans to women to rates of initiation and completion of graduate studies requires further study.

The relatively low proportion of women graduate students in the two decades before 1970 is currently reflected in their small representation on faculties (see Chapter 4) which may in turn create a less favorable learning environment for women students (Chapter 1). The need for maintenance of an adequately trained scientific work force, in view of declining enrollments (Table 2.2), suggests that more attention be devoted to the recruitment and retention of women graduate students.

Recruitment of women science students must also deal with the competition of professional training in law and medicine, which is attracting many of the ablest students, both women and men, but particularly women. The more limited job opportunities of the 1970's in the sciences have led to increased competition and lower confidence in scientific career prospects. A greater likelihood of being able to combine career and family responsibilities successfully in an independent profession may also contribute substantially to women's heightened interest in these fields. Unless better career prospects in science can be made evident to outstanding women students, they will have little incentive to pursue graduate training. The possibility that job openings in science may not expand and the near certainty that academic opportunities will contract make it more important to seek all of the best possible talent, not less.

In this chapter we look at the contenders at the start of their professional careers--young women and men just emerging from doctoral training--to see how evenly matched they are and whether they can fairly expect equal opportunities.

1. Comparative Quality of Women and Men at the Doctorate

No standard has yet been devised by which to measure the scientific promise of young researchers. Failing that, we use certain commonly measured characteristics such as grades and test scores, rank of institution or department granting the Ph.D., length of time taken to complete the degree (or its close relative, age), and stated future aspirations. All of these characteristics are open to a variety of interpretations: high grades may connote intellectual brilliance or mere diligence, average ones an average mind or an exceptional but unchallenged one; rapid completion of a thesis may be the result of luck as much as high motivation or inspired solutions. Nonetheless, the combination of intellectual ability, short time lapse to the Ph.D. (more commonly thought of as youth), and training at an outstanding department is generally thought of as a promising one.

A. Academic Ability

To the extent that grades and test scores are indicators of academic ability, women doctorates are a more promising group than men. Harmon found that for those in every field the high school grades, class rank, and standardized test scores of doctorate women far outranked those of comparable men (1965, pp. 28-32). Harmon's results are reproduced here in Figure 2.2.

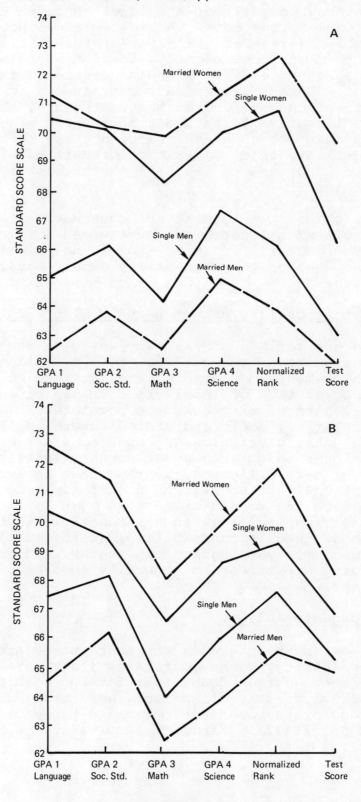

FIGURE 2.2 Profile of (A) Bioscientists and (B)
Social Scientists by Sex and Marital
Status at Doctorate, on Six High School
Variables

SOURCE: Harmon, 1965, pp. 31-32.

In the period covered by his work, careers in science were considered especially inappropriate for married women; the fact that married women appear at the top of the ability rankings of doctorate recipients at the same time that scientific careers were considered inappropriate for them supports the hypothesis that they were determined to succeed in the face of major obstacles.

The differences in mean ability between men and women doctorates that are illustrated here must be viewed in the context of the very different sizes of the two groups. Figure 2.2 shows that the distinctions are indeed less sharp among the social scientists, with larger ratios of women Ph.D.'s, than among biological scientists. As the number of all Ph.D.'s and the proportion of women Ph.D.'s has increased since the 1959-1962 period, a new study would indicate whether differences in ability patterns have narrowed.

A large-scale national study, the 1969 Carnegie Survey of Higher Education, found similar sex differences in the undergraduate grades of the graduate students in the study. It was found that 52 percent of the women graduate students, but only 37 percent of the men, had undergraduate grade point averages of B+ or better (Feldman, 1974, p. 18). The sex distribution of the GPA's is shown in Table 2.3. These findings are consistent with the greater degree of selectivity in women's admissions mentioned previously.

B.   Length of Study, and Age at Ph.D.

Elapsed time from baccalaureate to doctoral degree is very similar for male and female scientists and the differences have changed direction over the last ten years (Table 2.4). In several fields, women now take less time than men. Only in the medical sciences do women take substantially longer. In social sciences, psychology, and mathematics, women in the 1977 cohort showed less elapsed time than those of the 1967 cohort in completing their degrees. The trend is reversed for women in physics/astronomy. Men, however, increased the time from the earlier to the later cohort in nearly every field. The only field in which men reduced their B.A.-to-Ph.D. time lapse was the medical sciences, and this reduction accounts for most of the present difference between the sexes.

A similar pattern with respect to field differences and changes since the earlier period characterizes the median age of 1977 men and women doctorates (Table 2.5). In most fields, the differences in median age are small and favor women. The exceptions are psychology, in which the median age of women is slightly higher, and the medical sciences in which it is substantially higher.

TABLE 2.3   Percent Distribution of Undergraduate Grade Point Averages of Graduate
             Students by Sex*

	A+/A	A-	B+	B	B-	C+	C or below	Total	Weighted totals
Males	6.5	11.3	18.7	17.7	20.3	20.9	4.5	99.1	(178,932)
Females	6.7	18.1	26.7	18.6	17.1	11.3	1.6	100.1	(213,244)

*Gamma of sex differences = .236. Gamma is a measurement of the strength of a relation-
 ship between variables. The higher the gamma, the stronger the relationship. Gamma
 ranges from .00 (no relationship) to a maximum of 1.00 (absolute relationship).

Source: Feldman, 1974, pp. 16,18.

26

TABLE 2.4   Baccalaureate-to-Doctorate Time Lapse, by Field and Sex, 1967 and 1977 Science and Engineering Doctorates

Field of Doctorate	Men		Women	
	1967	1977	1967	1977
MEDIAN TIME LAPSE				
Mathematics	6.0 yrs.	6.9 yrs.	7.6 yrs.	7.2 yrs.
Physics/Astronomy	6.4	7.3	6.2	7.2
Chemistry	5.4	6.3	5.7	6.1
Earth Sciences	7.4	8.1	*	6.9
Engineering	7.2	7.5	*	6.4
Agriculture	8.0	8.2	*	8.0
Medical Sciences	8.4	7.0	8.8	8.9
Biological Sciences	6.8	7.0	7.1	7.1
Psychology	6.6	7.1	8.2	7.2
Social Sciences, including Psychology	7.5	8.1	9.1	7.9
25TH PERCENTILE				
Mathematics	4.6	5.2	5.2	5.7
Physics/Astronomy	5.2	5.8	5.3	6.0
Chemistry	4.4	5.0	4.7	5.0
Earth Sciences	5.6	6.2	*	5.4
Engineering	5.3	5.6	*	5.1
Agriculture	5.9	6.3	*	5.7
Medical Sciences	5.7	5.4	7.0	6.0
Biological Sciences	5.2	5.5	5.4	5.6
Psychology	5.0	5.4	5.7	5.4
Social Sciences	5.5	6.0	6.0	5.9

*Median not computed for fewer than 20 individuals.

Source: Doctorate Records File, National Research Council.

TABLE 2.5   Median Age at Ph.D. by Field and Sex, 1967 and 1977
Science and Engineering Doctorates

Field of Doctorate	Men		Women	
	1967	1977	1967	1977
Mathematics	28.1	29.1	29.7	29.0
Physics/Astronomy	28.6	29.5	27.5	29.1
Chemistry	27.7	28.6	28.0	28.2
Earth Sciences	30.4	30.7	*	29.1
Engineering	29.9	30.0	*	28.2
Agriculture	31.9	31.4	*	30.1
Medical Sciences	31.7	30.1	32.0	32.4
Biological Sciences	29.8	29.5	29.4	29.3
Psychology	29.8	29.8	31.1	30.0
Social Sciences, including Psychology	30.9	31.0	32.4	30.7

*Median not computed for fewer than 20 individuals reporting age.

Source: Doctorate Records File, National Research Council.

28

C. Institutional Origins of Doctorates

Male and female doctorates in each field are similarly distributed according to the institutions or departments in which they were trained. Table 2.6 compares the percentages of degrees granted to all doctorates and to women by all universities and by AAU universities[1] in two recent three-year periods, by broad fields. During the period from 1970 to 1972, in the life sciences, and more noticeably in the social sciences, a higher proportion of women than of all doctorates received degrees from AAU universities. There was no difference in the field of engineering while in the physical sciences, a smaller percentage of women than of all doctorates received degrees from AAU universities. For the later period, the picture had changed. In every field, a larger proportion of women Ph.D.'s than of all Ph.D.'s received their degrees at AAU universities. The difference was particularly marked in the field of engineering despite the small numbers of women involved.

A more detailed comparison of degrees granted in selected individual fields by departments rated highly by Roose-Andersen[2] is given in Table 2.7. In the six fields examined, the highest-rated departments produce major fractions of women Ph.D.'s, ranging from about one-third to one-half of the total. Table 2.7 illustrates some interesting differences among disciplines, which we shall see reflected later in employment figures (Chapters 3 and 4), as well as trends over time.

Before these differences and changes are described, it should be noted that with some variation, the percentages of both sexes trained by these highly rated departments dropped over the ten-year period, most notably in the case of psychology where graduate enrollments increased sharply in the decade. In mathematics, larger proportions of men than of women have been trained in highly rated departments and the difference has become slightly bigger as more women have gone into the field and pressures for equal access have mounted. With the exception of the initial period, highly rated physics departments have also trained larger percentages of male degree recipients. In contrast, prestigious microbiology and psychology departments have produced higher proportions of women than of men doctorates throughout the period, with the differences decreasing in recent years. High-ranking chemistry and sociology departments have fluctuated with both producing higher percentages of women than men Ph.D.'s for most of the ten-year period.

In the aggregate, given the relative numbers of degree recipients in the different fields, more women than men among recent science Ph.D.'s have received degrees at prestigious institutions. A much more detailed analysis,

29

TABLE 2.6 Science and Engineering Doctorates Granted in 1970-1972 and 1973-1975 by All U.S. Universities and by AAU Universities*, by Field, All Degrees and Degrees Granted to Women

	Total Degrees			Degrees Granted		
	All Univ. No.	AAU No.	AAU %	All Univ. No.	AAU No.	AAU %
1970-1972						
Physical Sciences	16,902	10,193	60.3	1,028	591	57.5
Engineering	10,436	6,428	61.6	52	32	61.5
Life Sciences	14,594	6,089	41.7	2,034	895	44.0
Social Sciences	15,340	8,334	54.3	2,706	1,650	61.0
1973-1975						
Physical Sciences	15,134	9,026	59.6	1,169	734	62.8
Engineering	9,511	5,484	57.7	131	93	71.0
Life Sciences	14,742	6,012	40.8	2,685	1,166	43.4
Social Sciences	18,413	9,197	49.9	4,290	2,318	54.0

*Universities that are members of the Association of American Universities.

Source: Data on degrees granted by AAU universities are from "Doctorates Granted to Women and Minority Group Members," by Joseph L. McCarthy and Dael Wolfle, Science, Vol. 189, Sept. 12, 1975, p.856. Data on degrees granted by all universities are from the Survey of Earned Doctorates, published in Gilford & Syverson, p.8.

TABLE 2.7 Number and Percent of Doctorates Granted in Selected Science Fields by Highly-Ranked Departments*, Out of All Departments, by Sex and Two-Year Period, 1967-1977

Field of Doctorate		1967 & 1968 Men	1967 & 1968 Women	1969 & 1970 Men	1969 & 1970 Women	1971 & 1972 Men	1971 & 1972 Women	1973 & 1974 Men	1973 & 1974 Women	1975 & 1976 Men	1975 & 1976 Women	1977 Men	1977 Women
Physics/ Astronomy	No.	1,390	54	1,454	33	1,535	41	1,289	49	1,077	48	502	28
	%	52.0	76.1	48.1	39.3	47.0	40.2	45.8	43.4	44.7	38.4	46.3	43.8
Chemistry	No.	1,633	138	1,786	159	1,740	159	1,422	158	1,335	182	623	68
	%	49.3	53.5	46.1	48.3	45.2	42.1	43.2	44.4	44.2	47.5	44.8	37.8
Microbiology	No.	197	65	200	75	174	66	161	80	156	71	74	31
	%	35.4	47.4	32.4	45.5	27.2	40.2	28.5	40.4	29.2	37.2	32.7	36.0
Sociology	No.	287	65	347	97	395	104	376	162	391	189	191	88
	%	50.5	49.2	46.9	56.1	40.7	41.1	41.5	47.8	39.9	43.6	39.1	37.1
Psychology	No.	894	292	1,018	364	1,089	490	1,114	575	1,080	631	501	320
	%	41.4	48.9	36.5	42.5	33.3	43.2	31.5	37.9	28.3	34.7	26.7	29.6
Mathematics	No.	865	44	1,002	54	1,039	83	994	97	906	87	372	49
	%	50.7	46.3	46.5	40.6	44.6	43.2	45.0	41.5	47.0	39.2	44.8	38.3

*Roose-Andersen rating. For an explanation of the rating and the lists of the highly-rated institutions in each field, see Appendix B-2.

Source: Survey of Earned Doctorates, National Research Council.

31

well beyond the scope of this report, is needed to identify reasons for the divergent sex ratios in some fields among highly rated departments including, especially, evaluations of applications in relation to admissions, and analysis of retention patterns of graduate students. Such a study would be of general interest in establishing whether practices in certain fields are systematically sex-biased.

2. Plans for Postdoctoral Study

Planning postdoctoral study has traditionally been a measure of high aspirations but may now also reflect realistic assessments of a tight job market. The fact that men and women plan to embark on postdoctoral training in comparable proportions, field by field, is therefore an indication of general similarity in their professional aspirations although they may pursue this training for different reasons. A more detailed analysis of this topic follows in Chapter 3.

3. Labor Force Participation and Unemployment

We mentioned earlier that women account for 10.4 percent of all science and engineering doctorates awarded since 1920 (Table 2.1). How similar is their presence in the work force, the work force being the effective supply of women doctorates?

Table 2.8 shows that in 1977, 9.7 percent of the doctoral work force were women. Their participation varies greatly by field, from nearly one fourth in psychology to less than one percent in engineering.

While women comprised 10 percent of the doctoral work force in 1975, they accounted for nearly 30 percent of the Ph.D.'s who were unemployed involuntarily or who took part-time positions because full-time jobs were not available. Table 2.9 shows that women were three times more likely than men to be unemployed and seeking employment. The sex differences in unemployment rates were greatest among physicists. In all fields, the proportions of women who were unemployed and seeking work, or part-time employed and seeking full-time employment exceeded those for men (Maxfield, Ahern, and Spisak, 1976, p. 8).

4. Marital Status

Certain factors which have no bearing on quality of doctorates and no intrinsic relationship to prospects for general professional success may nonetheless legitimately affect relative employment prospects.

One of the factors most frequently cited to affect the education, employment status, and professional achievement

TABLE 2.8   Number and Percent of Women Doctoral Scientists and Engineers in the Labor Force by Field, 1977

Field of Doctorate	Number of Women	Percent of Women
All Science & Engineering Fields	27,282	9.7
Math/Computer Sciences	1,151	6.9
Physics/Astronomy	646	2.5
Chemistry	2,551	6.1
Earth Sciences	332	3.6
Engineering	231	0.5
Life Sciences		
Agricultural	261	2.0
Medical	1,018	13.3
Biological	7,742	15.6
Psychology	7,543	23.1
Social Sciences	5,807	14.0

Source: Survey of Doctorate Recipients, National Research Council. The statistics in this table are weighted estimates derived from a sample survey of 65,000 Ph.D.'s in science and engineering. The estimates are subject to two types of error -- sampling and nonsampling, (e.g., nonresponse bias). A discussion of the survey is provided in Appendix D.

TABLE 2.9   1975 Employment Status by Field of Doctorate and Sex

| Field of Doctorate | Labor Force | | Employment Status[+] | | | | | |
| | | | Unemployed, Seeking Work | | Full-Time Nonscience Employed Because Science Position Not Available | | Part-Time Employed and Seeking Full-Time | |
	Male	Female	Male	Female	Male	Female	Male	Female
All Fields[#]	N	N	%	%	%	%	%	%
1973	211,343	18,049	0.9	3.9	0.3	0.3	0.7	3.5
1975	242,346	23,188	0.8	3.0	0.3	0.4	0.5	2.4
Mathematics								
1973	12,132	777	1.4	1.9	0.2	.0	0.4	2.4
1975	14,400	979	0.5	1.9	0.4	0.5	0.6	2.2
Physics/Astronomy								
1973	20,878	453	1.4	6.8	0.6	.0	1.1	8.4
1975	23,494	546	1.5	7.3	0.6	0.9	0.8	2.7
Chemistry								
1973	34,838	1,837	1.4	6.5	0.5	0.2	0.8	3.9
1975	38,481	2,212	0.9	3.7	0.5	0.5	0.4	2.8
Earth Sciences								
1973	7,066	171	0.7	2.9	0.1	.0	0.6	9.4
1975	8,278	247	1.0	3.2	0.2	0.4	0.5	1.2
Engineering								
1973	33,872	114	0.8	6.1	0.2	1.8	0.5	4.4
1975	40,183	170	0.7	2.4	0.2	.0	0.3	0.6
Biosciences								
1973	50,594	6,071	0.6	4.5	0.2	0.5	0.5	3.2
1975	58,258	7,751	0.7	3.6	0.1	0.4	0.5	1.8
Psychology								
1973	18,262	4,417	0.7	3.1	0.1	0.2	0.4	3.8
1975	22,218	6,062	0.6	1.7	0.2	0.3	0.6	2.5
Social Sciences								
1973	26,704	3,053	0.7	2.8	0.3	0.3	0.9	3.3
1975	32,724	4,415	0.6	3.3	0.3	0.4	0.6	3.2
Nonsciences								
1973	6,851	1,131	0.7	2.6	.0	.0	0.5	1.9
1975	4,155	782	0.3	1.2	.0	.0	*	1.0

[+]Percentage of Labor Force in Survey Year
[#]Includes those not Reporting Field of Ph.D.
*Less Than 0.1%

SOURCE: Maxfield, Ahern, and Spisak, 1976, p.8.

of women is marital status. Marriage-career incompatibility for women has been given as the explanation for the much smaller percentage of women than men doctorates who are married. The percentages, by field, for 1977 Ph.D.'s are displayed in Table 2.10.

It is apparent that in most fields, more men than women Ph.D.'s are married at the time they receive the degree. The field of physics and astronomy is the exception with a higher proportion of married women, and the percentages of married men and women are almost identical in mathematics and engineering. The biggest sex differences are found in the medical and agricultural sciences which have high proportions of married men and low proportions of married women.

It should be pointed out that answers to a question on marital status may not accurately describe informal arrangements that are now quite common in the graduate student population. It is known that the proportion of married men has been steadily dropping among U.S.-born doctorates in recent years, but not among new women Ph.D.'s (Gilford and Snyder, 1977, p. 36), but we do not know whether traditional marriages are being supplanted by such informal arrangements. Nor do we know how these commitments may affect the educational and career choices of Ph.D.'s of either sex.

The data likewise do not reveal past marital ties of those receiving the doctorate. All studies have shown high rates of separation and divorce among women graduate students (e.g., Feldman, 1974, p. 19) and women doctorates (e.g., Centra, 1974, p. 103) so that many who report themselves as single when they receive the degree may have been married earlier. Data on 1973-1976 women Ph.D.'s showed nearly 30 percent to have at least one dependent when they obtained the Ph.D. (Gilford and Snyder, 1977, p. 38). This requires consideration in the award of stipends for the postdoctoral training of women Ph.D.'s.

Marital status has been identified as a crucial factor operating to reduce the retention of women in college (Astin, 1969, p. 18), the likelihood that they will attend graduate school (Cross, 1973, pp. 46-47), the time they spend on professional activity (Centra, 1974, p. 43), and their productivity as measured by number of publications (Centra, 1974, p. 77).

Marriage is also assumed to act as a barrier to the geographical mobility required for professional advancement. There is some evidence to support this assumption. In the Centra comparison of men and women Ph.D.'s of different cohorts (1974), 49 percent of the women reported that the spouse's job had been a major deterrent to their

TABLE 2.10 Number and Percent of 1977 Science and Engineering
Doctorate Recipients Who Were Married at Receipt of
the Doctorate, by Field and Sex

Field of Doctorate	Men		Women	
	No.	%	No.	%
All Science/Engr. Fields	10,069	67.2	1,691	51.4
Physics & Astronomy	659	60.7	44	68.8
Chemistry	870	62.6	94	52.2
Earth Sciences	457	72.3	31	52.5
Mathematics	489	58.8	73	57.0
Engineering	1,738	67.7	49	66.2
Biological Sciences	1,665	68.2	365	50.1
Medical Sciences	365	72.1	80	48.5
Agriculture	684	79.4	27	42.9
Psychology	1,183	63.0	546	50.5
Social Sciences	3,142	67.2	928	50.7

Source: Survey of Earned Doctorates, National Research Council

consideration of a job that would require a move to another community, in comparison with 4 percent of the men. Among the women who reported having experienced periods of unemployment, 57 percent of the reasons they gave concerned marital status and family responsibilities, but none of the men who had been without work at some time after receipt of the degree gave such reasons. A 1976 survey of 1971-1975 Ph.D.'s in the biomedical and behavioral sciences found that married women in both fields were somewhat more likely than single men or women, or married men, to have spent time unemployed following the degree and to be seeking employment at the time of the survey (NRC, 1977, Vol. 2, pp. 133-134).[3] Their higher unemployment rate might suggest that married women could afford to be more selective about the jobs they accepted, but other results of the study show that this is not the case. In the same study, married women were much more likely than the other groups to state that their degrees were irrelevant to their current employment (p. 139).

In any event, many of the reported differences between married and single women with respect to professional employment and achievement are not large. In a number of studies, married women show some differences when compared with the members of the other categories but they are not at the present time _very_ different from single men and women Ph.D.'s. The same may be said of the differences reported in Chapter 3 for their postdoctoral status, and for their tenure standing and salaries (Chapter 4). In fact, the group that displays major differences in these respects consists of married men. They are the ones least likely to plan or to hold postdoctoral appointments and the group most likely to achieve tenure or be in tenure-track positions early in their careers. In the Centra study, married men published at nearly double the rate of single men or women or married women (p. 77).

It is probable that economic responsibilities of married men account for somewhat distinctive educational and employment patterns. For example, in the Carnegie survey, married male graduate students were more likely than single males, or single or married females, to list increased earning power as a motive for attending graduate school (Feldman, 1974, p. 129). If postdoctoral study has traditionally been a measure of high aspiration or the road for men to professional advancement (Reskin, 1976), it appears to be a luxury that many married men cannot afford. Family responsibilities may also help to explain the greater proportion of men than women doctorates who are employed in industry where salaries are higher than in other work sectors (Chapter 4).

We also know from Astin's study of women doctorates (1969, p. 28) and Centra's comparison of men and women

37

Ph.D.'s that 63 percent of the husbands of married women Ph.D.'s had doctorates or professional degrees in comparison with 8.3 percent of the wives of the men doctorates. In the same survey, 90 percent of the husbands of the married women Ph.D.'s had been employed full time or almost full time since the marriage, as compared with 12 percent of the wives of the men Ph.D.'s. Ths would again indicate a greater burden of family support on the men Ph.D.'s.

Several possible explanations for the greater "success rate" of married men suggest themselves. One is simply that they are better than other individuals, a deduction which finds little support in studies of ability patterns (see, for example, Figure 2.2 and Tables 2.3 and 2.4). Another is that the need to provide for a family provides added motivation; conversely, educational and career structures may also respond to this need. Finally, the supporting labor of a wife may free a man of other responsibilities and leave him more freedom to pursue work-related interests.

Conclusions

Men and women scientists at receipt of the doctorate are similar in average quality although women have an edge in academic ability as measured by college grades and high school test scores. In engineering and in most science fields, they receive their Ph.D. at the same age or younger than men, and have completed their training as fast or faster than men. Generally, similar proportions of both sexes are trained at highly-rated institutions. Based on the evidence presented here, one would expect the prospective opportunities for career development of young men and women doctorates to be essentially equal.

Recommendations

Three more detailed studies are recommended to assess the sex distribution in admissions to highly-rated graduate departments, differences in graduate training patterns depending on B.A. origins, and influence of marital status on employment prospects:

1. A detailed analysis of graduate admissions patterns, by field and sex, in prestigious departments; this should analyze trends over the last decade and establish a design for annual monitoring in the next few years.

2. A study of the graduate training patterns of women who earned baccalaureates from formerly all-male (or predominantly male) colleges and universities

to determine whether these patterns differ significantly from those of alumnae of other institutions.

3. A study of the relationship between marital status, geographic mobility, and postdoctoral employment status of women, using data from the Doctorate Records File. Analysis of the effect of marital status on professional employment during later career periods will require the addition of a question on marital status to the Survey of Doctorate Recipients.

NOTES

1   AAU universities are those belonging to the Association of American Universities. Membership includes most major research universities and is taken as a measure of quality although, for some universities, that rating may have changed since the period when membership was acquired.

2   See Appendix B-2 for these ratings.

3   A survey of recent Ph.D. recipients in the biomedical and behavioral fields conducted by the Committee on a Study of National Needs for Biomedical and Behavioral Research Personnel of the Commission on Human Resources, National Research Council.

CHAPTER 3

POSTDOCTORAL TRAINING

Once limited to a few young scientists of exceptional promise, postdoctoral training has increased dramatically in both the natural and social sciences over the past twenty years, (NRC, 1974c, p. 30) although the rates of increase vary substantially by discipline. Several observers have noted that the increasing popularity of postdoctoral appointments is inversely related to the availability of regular positions, especially tenure-track faculty posts [Cartter, 1971; NRC, 1969; NRC, 1971; Wilsnack, 1977]. Conversely, the availability of postdoctoral positions varies considerably with the amount of research support available in a given field or year.

Because research support comes very largely from Federal sources, and because noncompliance with equal opportunity policies threatens withdrawal of such support, science departments which are potentially most vulnerable to such a loss should furnish good test cases for examining recent sex patterns. For that reason, we examine several factors in postdoctoral training (and in faculty employment in Chapter 4) by grouping institutions according to Federal R&D expenditures.

The traditional benefits of postdoctoral study include freedom to do research without the pressures inherent in either graduate study or a first job, the expansion of research horizons, an opportunity to establish or expand publication records, and the broadening of professional contacts and personal exposure. A consequence of these benefits for postdoctoral fellows is the increased likelihood of holding tenure-track faculty posts at research universities (Folger et al., 1970, p. 249; NRC, 1974c, p. 65-69). But such consequences may not follow equally for men and women, and a more detailed examination of what happens to women as postdoctorals is therefore important. Some older studies may serve as background to consideration of these issues.

The largest of these, The Invisible University (NRC, 1969) treated women scientists themselves as almost invisible, reporting briefly that they received

substantially lower stipends than men, remained long-term
postdoctorals about three times as often, could not expect
to hold regular faculty appointments, and were therefore
happy to hold any kind of postdoctoral position [pp. 70,
105, 117-118, 135, 226]. All inequities were uniformly
ascribed to family constraints, although nearly half the
female population in the study was unmarried.

Although women constituted one-tenth of the postdoctoral
population under study (computed from NRC, 1969, Table 27,
p. 105), the report did not consider how the postdoctoral
experience affected them, whether it was significantly
different from that of men, or even whether the money spent
on them was well invested. The data upon which the report
was based were coded by sex, marital status, and number of
dependents, but not analyzed to ascertain the differential
effects of these variables on stipends or career
opportunities. The report is therefore of very limited
usefulness for our purposes.

Reanalysis of this body of data to establish
relationships between sex and marital status, type of
postdoctoral appointment, stipends, length of time in
postdoctoral training, and subsequent positions held would
furnish an important bench mark for comparison with future
studies. We strongly urge that such a reanalysis be
undertaken.

The second major study of postdoctoral training (NRC,
1974c), again collected data by sex (and certain performance
measures were standardized by sex; pp. 118-119), but
analyses in the body of the report were not broken down by
sex, and this report added little to our knowledge of the
experience of female postdoctorals.

There is some evidence that female scientists were more
likely than males to have postdoctoral training (NRC, 1968,
p. 81; Reskin, 1976, p. 607), but more complex data for more
disciplines are necessary to permit generalizations about
sex differences.

The importance of postdoctoral training for the
individual lies in the direct enhancement of careers, and
the only major study of this effect which has been
undertaken, for the field of chemistry, (Reskin, 1973 and
1976) gave very different results for men and women.
Although the women were more likely to have had postdoctoral
fellowships than the men, the male fellows received
substantially more prestigious awards. Such indicators of
predoctoral quality as caliber of undergraduate institution,
prestige of doctoral department, elapsed time from
baccalaureate, or productivity of Ph.D. sponsor were found
to be significantly related to prestige of the postdoctoral
award for men, but unrelated for women. In particular,

selectivity of the B.A. institution and predoctoral publications increased award prestige greatly for men but not for women.

Careers of sample members were traced for 10-15 years after the Ph.D. (through 1970). The results showed that the receipt of a postdoctoral award and its prestige facilitated the male chemists' careers in the expected manner (e.g., increased their likelihood of holding a tenured university appointment), but had no effect on the women's occupational outcome. This finding is especially significant in view of the fact that the subsequent scientific productivity (measured by both number of articles and citations) of both sexes was enhanced by postdoctoral training. Thus women, like men, profited from their postdoctoral training, but unlike men they could not convert their subsequent superior performance to permanent jobs as university faculty. In a larger study of the same chemists (Reskin, 1973) it was found that women's productivity over their first ten years after receiving the Ph.D. was generally unrelated to the positions they held at that time although men's performance and occupational position were positively related.

These results concerning an earlier period are cited here primarily to underline the traditional importance of postdoctoral training for men and illustrate the fact that at least in the past women were unlikely to realize the same benefits. We do not yet have a sufficiently long perspective on recent postdoctorals to know whether these inequities persist, or to what extent. An understanding of the ways in which women's careers differed in detail from men's in the past, even with an equal or better start, can serve to highlight the factors which need to be monitored in the future in relation to the outcomes of postdoctoral training.

The presence of postdoctoral fellows or research associates also has important benefits for the research groups they join, increasing the group's overall research output and adding new or different capabilities. These benefits accrue most markedly to the group's mentor, and ideally a symbiotic relationship exists between the mentor and postdoctoral fellow (NRC, 1969). Based on Reskin's study dealing with chemistry, women postdoctorals may not have been viewed in the past as promising disciples because of their much lower likelihood of obtaining positions which would permit them to carry on independent research careers (Reskin, 1976; see also Chapter 4) or to achieve other kinds of professional recognition (Chapter 5). This perception may in turn lessen the help and attention they receive from their postdoctoral mentors. New studies, such as the one in progress by the Committee on the Study of Postdoctorals and Doctoral Research Staff of the Commission on Human

Resources, should endeavor to assess these rather subtle issues.

The Current Patterns of Postdoctoral Appointments

At the present time, similar proportions of men and women doctorates plan postdoctoral study though there is considerable variation by field. Table 3.1 shows the percentages of 1977 Ph.D.'s in each field planning such training, as well as percentages of those with definite appointments and those still seeking or negotiating contracts. If we examine similar data for several years we find predictable fluctuations in those fields where women are very poorly represented, and where those interested in postdoctoral work may comprise only a few individuals.

It is clear from Table 3.1 that in general, high proportions of doctorates in the biological and physical sciences, excluding mathematics, take such positions. Earth sciences displays somewhat lower proportions than the other physical sciences while engineering shows still lower percentages. Mathematics is in sharp contrast to the other EMP fields in that there are few postdoctoral positions. In psychology, the percentage is relatively low and the social sciences reflect still smaller figures. It is apparent that the requirements of each field that encourage work at this level and the opportunities for postdoctoral study vary widely.

A tabulation by sex and marital status of the 1970-1977 degree recipients who were planning postdoctoral study at the time they received their degrees sheds further light on factors associated with postdoctoral study (Table 3.2). As indicated earlier (Chapter 2), married men are the group least likely to plan such appointments. This holds true for doctorates as a whole and in each field except mathematics. The NRC survey of biomedical and behavioral scientists found a similar pattern among 1971-1975 degree holders in these fields: lower proportions of married men held such appointments at any time after the degree or at the time of the study (1976). The married men in both fields who had held such appointments were far more likely than single men or women, and somewhat more likely than married women, to give as a reason for having undertaken postdoctoral work the inability to find a job, as opposed to the goal of obtaining research experience or switching fields (NRC, 1977, Vol. 2, pp. 133-135). The comparison of postdoctoral stipends with the salaries offered in the various employment sectors, presented in Table 4.21 of this report, in relation to the assumed financial responsibilities of married men makes this finding understandable. Thus the lower incidence of postdoctorals among married men is probably due to societal pressures on this group for greater earnings.

TABLE 3.1   Number and Percent of 1977 Science and Engineering Doctorate
Recipients Planning Postdoctoral Appointments by Field and
Sex

Field of Doctorate

	Men		Women	
	No.	%	No.	%
Total Planning Postdoc				
All Fields	3956	26.3	1260	14.3
Math	95	11.4	11	8.6
Physics/Astronomy	503	46.4	33	51.5
Chemistry	645	46.4	91	50.6
Earth Sciences	157	24.8	22	37.3
Engineering	380	14.8	12	16.3
Agricultural Sci.	110	12.7	13	20.6
Medical Sciences	201	39.7	61	37.0
Biological Sciences	1410	57.7	449	61.5
Psychology	301	16.0	162	15.0
Social Sciences	455	9.8	221	12.1
Definite Postdoc				
All Fields	2945	19.6	664	20.2
Math	61	7.3	3	2.3
Physics/Astronomy	372	34.3	18	28.1
Chemistry	498	35.8	68	37.8
Earth Sciences	112	17.7	18	30.5
Engineering	234	9.1	7	9.5
Agricultural Sci.	70	8.1	7	11.1
Medical Sciences	158	31.2	50	30.3
Biological Sciences	1137	46.5	351	48.1
Psychology	210	11.2	105	9.7
Social Sciences	303	6.5	142	7.8
Seeking Postdoc				
All Fields	1011	6.7	249	7.6
Math	34	4.1	8	6.3
Physics/Astronomy	131	12.1	15	23.4
Chemistry	147	10.6	23	12.8
Earth Sciences	45	7.1	4	6.8
Engineering	146	5.7	5	6.8
Agricultural Sci.	40	4.6	6	9.5
Medical Sciences	43	8.5	11	6.7
Biological Sciences	273	11.2	98	13.4
Psychology	91	4.8	57	5.3
Social Sciences	152	3.3	79	4.3

Source: Gilford and Syverson, 1978, pp. 22-25.

TABLE 3.2   Percent of 1970-1977 Science and Engineering Doctorate Recipients
Planning Postdoctoral Study After Graduation by Field, Sex, and
Marital Status

Field of Doctorate	Married Women	Unmarried Women	Married Men	Unmarried Men
All Fields	30.2%	31.4%	22.8%	35.3%
Mathematics	8.0	4.2	6.3	12.8
Physics/Astronomy	47.6	61.8	42.1	59.3
Chemistry	54.1	53.4	43.6	61.4
Earth Sciences	33.7	36.8	20.1	32.9
Engineering	14.9	11.6	9.6	19.3
Agricultural Sci.	32.9	23.9	12.2	26.0
Medical/Biological Sci.	61.5	57.9	48.6	67.9
Psychology	14.5	18.3	12.5	18.9
Social Sciences	6.3	6.3	3.6	5.5

* Percent based on total number of Ph.D. recipients who either had
  definite commitments or were negotiating contracts at the time of
  graduation.

Source: Survey of Earned Doctorates, 1970-1977, National Research Council.
Interim Report to National Science Foundation and Proposal for
Continuation of Study of Postdoctorals in Science and Engineering
in the United States. June 29, 1978, p. 76.

In contrast, on the whole and in nearly every field, single men are most likely to plan postdoctoral work (Table 3.2). Why they should make this choice more frequently than single or married women is not obvious. Nor, without a closer examination of each field, can the exceptions be explained: the higher proportions of single women in physics and earth sciences and of married women in agricultural sciences.

Table 3.3 illustrates recent trends in the sex composition of the postdoctoral population as well as the changes that have occurred at institutions of different rank in the sciences as a whole and in two fields. Except for a very slight decline among the top 25 institutions in 1977, there is a steady rise in the proportion of women at the postdoctoral level. Similar results are found for the individual fields of chemistry and biosciences which consistently have postdoctoral populations that are large enough to be examined in this way.

Table 3.3 also shows that in the biosciences, the proportions of women postdoctorals have been and continue to be larger at the lowest-ranked institutions, but this has not been the case in chemistry. The greater concentration of women in "all other" institutions throughout the 1973-1977 period is largely accounted for by women in the biosciences who make up the great majority of all women postdoctoral appointees (see Table 3.4). The percentage increase of women in the biological sciences during this period has, however, been smaller at low-ranking institutions than among the top 25.

Table 3.4 illustrates the changes in the proportions of women at the postdoctoral level in a different way by showing the percentages by fields of the members of each sex employed in academic institutions who were in postdoctoral positions in 1973 and 1977. Proportions of women increased in all fields except medical sciences. In several fields with very few women—physics/astronomy, earth sciences, engineering, and agricultural sciences—the percentages of women increased markedly over the four-year period so that there was a substantial difference between the sexes in 1977 but it should be noted that the numbers are very small. A similar pattern was observed in the social sciences, a field in which there are very few postdoctorals of either sex. In chemistry and biology, the fields with the largest numbers of postdoctorals, the proportions of women were larger than those of men in 1973 and the difference increased in 1977.

The acceptances of men and women applying for postdoctorals are illustrated in Table 3.5. Shown are the total number of new Ph.D.'s who desired postdoctoral appointments (i.e., fellowships, traineeships, research associateships, etc.) and the percentage of those who had

TABLE 3.3   Trends in Number and Percent of Women Among Postdoctorals in Science and Engineering by Field of Doctorate and R&D Expenditures of Post-doctoral Institution*, 1973-1977

	1973		1975		1977	
	No.	%	No.	%	No.	%
ALL SCIENCE/ENGR. FIELDS						
Top 25 Inst.	209	11.7	301	18.9	387	17.4
Second 25 Inst.	124	14.1	162	16.6	200	18.9
All other Inst.	443	17.6	763	21.7	951	22.5
CHEMISTRY[+]						
Top 25 Inst.	48	13.8	47	13.4	75	20.4
Second 25 Inst.	29	15.8	24	12.1	36	18.8
All Other Inst.	49	9.3	95	15.1	104	15.8
BIOLOGICAL SCIENCES[+]						
Top 25 Inst.	120	17.9	156	27.6	199	23.0
Second 25 Inst.	70	17.1	95	25.3	133	26.3
All Other Inst.	311	27.9	459	27.0	622	32.2

* See Appendix B-1 for a description of ranking of institutions by R&D expenditures.

[+] For fields other than chemistry and biological sciences, the number of postdoctoral appointees was not sufficient to permit a break-out by institution group and sex.

Source: Survey of Doctorate Recipients, National Research Council. The statistics in this table are weighted estimates derived from a sample survey of 65,000 Ph.D's in science and engineering. The estimates are subject to two types of error -- sampling and non-sampling, (e.g., non-response bias). A discussion of the survey is provided in Appendix D.

TABLE 3.4   Trends in Number and Percent of Doctoral Scientists and
            Engineers in Academe Who Were on Postdoctorals by
            Field and Sex, 1973-1977

Field	1973 MALE		1973 FEMALE		1977 MALE		1977 FEMALE	
	No.	%	No.	%	No.	%	No.	%
Mathematics	47	0.5	4	0.6	47	0.5	6	0.7
Physics/Astronomy	766	8.9	23	8.8	638	6.9	34	12.0
Chemistry	935	9.9	126	16.3	1005	8.7	215	18.0
Earth Sciences	154	3.3	8	5.3	261	4.8	30	12.0
Engineering	339	2.9	0	0	337	2.5	12	13.2
Agricultural Sciences	65	1.1	*	*	150	1.9	19	13.5
Medical Sciences	289	6.1	62	9.8	670	9.8	113	9.6
Bio Sciences	1693	7.8	501	15.0	2350	9.8	954	19.6
Psychology	120	1.3	28	1.4	262	2.3	87	2.8
Social Sciences	150	0.8	22	1.1	217	0.9	68	1.8

* Estimates based on fewer than 3 sample individuals are not shown.

Source: Survey of Doctorate Recipients, National Research Council
          The statistics in this table are weighted estimates derived
          from a sample survey of 65,000 Ph.D's in science and engineering.
          The estimates are subject to two types of error - sampling and
          non-sampling, (e.g., non-response bias). A discussion of the
          survey is provided in Appendix D.

49

signed contracts or awards at the time of Ph.D. It should
be noted that in some fields there are wide year-to-year
fluctuations due to small numbers.

In chemistry and biological sciences—the fields with
the largest numbers of postdoctorals—rates of awards to
women over the past decade have been consistently lower than
for men, although the differences are not large.

Physics shows no improvement in relative awards to women
since the advent of affirmative action, and this pattern
coincides with what is perhaps the weakest employment
prospect of all science fields. However, in the medical
sciences, the comparative figures favor women in 1977.

Holding Status

An issue that has long been posed with respect to women
postdoctorals is whether, in fact, they remain in these
appointments in a kind of "holding status" because they
cannot find any other employment or because they are
prevented by marital ties from moving elsewhere to look for
jobs. This was the assumption clearly stated in The
Invisible University (NRC, 1969, pp. 70, 118). In the only
detailed analysis of sex differences in postdoctoral
experience, Reskin's study of 1955-1961 Ph.D.'s in chemistry
found that women, and particularly married women, were
indeed more likely than men to have held multiple
appointments and to have held these longer (1976, pp. 608-
609). The recent NRC survey of 1971-1975 biomedical and
behavioral science Ph.D.'s, however, did not find this
pattern. Although breakdowns of the data were not made by
marital status or other factors, men in the behavioral
sciences were much more likely, and in the biomedical fields
somewhat more likely, than women to have had their
postdoctoral appointments prolonged or to have held them for
more than 36 months (NRC, 1977b, Vol. 2, pp. 31, 78).
Again, we need an updated and detailed analysis by field of
the experiences of men and women at the postdoctoral level.

Postdoctoral Stipends

Stipends are an important measure of equity for several
reasons. Inequities at this level may contribute to
disadvantages in subsequent salaries. Further, systematic
inequities are harder to uncover here than in readily
visible criteria such as rank because salary information
frequently remains private.

Postdoctoral stipends are also subject to the normal
economics of supply and demand, and to the exigencies of
research support, so that they may vary quite significantly

TABLE 3.5 Percent of Science and Engineering Doctorate Recipients with Signed Contract for Postdoctoral Appointment,* by Field, Year of Doctorate and Sex, 1969-1977

	Men Postdoctorals				Women Postdoctorals			
	Total Planning Post-doctoral	No. Seeking	No. Signed	% With Signed Contract	Total Planning Post-doctoral	No. Seeking	No. Signed	% With Signed Contract
Mathematics								
1969	85	17	68	80%	3	1	2	67%
1971	82	23	59	72	7	3	4	57
1973	102	30	72	71	13	2	11	85
1975	106	31	75	71	8	4	4	50
1977	93	32	61	66	11	8	3	27
Total	468	133	335	72	42	18	24	57
Physics/ Astr.								
1969	498	98	400	80%	16	6	10	62%
1971	651	143	508	78	19	5	14	74
1973	684	168	516	75	29	10	19	66
1975	576	148	428	74	31	10	21	68
1977	499	127	372	74	31	13	18	58
Total	2,908	684	2,224	76	126	44	82	65
Chemistry								
1969	593	71	522	88%	48	8	40	83%
1971	869	122	747	86	80	20	60	75
1973	832	179	653	78	75	30	45	60
1975	720	121	599	83	87	26	61	70
1977	632	134	498	79	90	22	68	76
Total	3,646	627	3,019	83	380	106	274	72
Earth Sciences								
1969	87	18	69	79%	6	3	3	50%
1971	108	27	81	75	3	-	3	100
1973	138	47	91	66	10	3	7	70
1975	131	35	96	73	7	2	5	71
1977	155	43	112	72	22	4	18	82
Total	619	170	449	72	48	12	36	75
Engineering								
1969	221	68	153	69%	-	-	-	-
1971	385	152	233	60	1	-	1	100%
1973	462	169	293	63	10	5	5	50
1975	376	149	227	60	6	3	3	50
1977	265	131	234	38	12	5	7	58
Total	1,709	669	1,140	67	29	13	16	55

*Postdoctoral appointment includes a postdoctoral fellowship, research associateship traineeship, or other study.

TABLE 3.5 (Continued)

	Men Postdoctorals				Women Postdoctorals			
	Total Planning Post-doctoral	No. Seeking	No. Signed	% With Signed Contract	Total Planning Post-doctoral	No. Seeking	No. Signed	% With Signed Contract
Agricultural Sciences								
1969	99	32	67	68%	3	2	1	33%
1971	132	48	84	64	9	4	5	56
1973	164	64	100	61	8	3	5	62
1975	145	51	94	65	7	3	4	57
1977	106	36	70	66	13	6	7	54
Total	646	231	415	64	40	18	22	55
Medical Sciences								
1969	112	16	96	86%	15	4	11	73%
1971	136	20	116	85	25	6	19	76
1973	136	24	112	82	33	3	30	91
1975	157	21	136	87	32	5	27	84
1977	198	40	158	80	59	9	50	85
Total	739	121	618	84	164	27	137	84
Biological Sciences								
1969	926	131	795	86%	232	41	191	82%
1971	1,301	218	1,083	83	279	63	216	77
1973	1,245	228	1,017	82	371	87	284	76
1975	1,308	230	1,078	82	471	97	374	79
1977	1,386	249	1,137	82	444	93	351	79
Total	6,166	1,056	5,110	83	1,797	381	1,416	79
Psychology								
1969	168	30	138	82%	48	9	39	81%
1971	218	35	183	84	78	18	60	77
1973	201	46	155	77	98	24	74	76
1975	246	61	185	75	129	31	98	76
1977	293	83	210	72	155	50	105	68
Total	1,126	255	871	77	508	132	376	74
Social Sciences								
1969	77	17	60	78%	4	2	2	50%
1971	82	24	58	71	19	10	9	47
1973	145	40	105	72	24	10	14	58
1975	95	34	61	64	48	22	26	54
1977	147	54	93	63	57	20	37	65
Total	546	169	377	69	152	64	88	58

Source: Survey of Earned Doctorates, National Research Council.

from year to year, field to field, or even project to project. When groups of reasonable size within a particular field are compared, however, their salaries would not be expected to differ significantly in the absence of group biases.

Such comparisons are not easy to generate for postdoctoral fellows, and information from previous studies is not abundant. About a decade ago, women postdoctorals were reported to earn an average of about $1400 less than men (NAS, 1969). Table 3.6 shows that the large differential narrowed since then, but now appears to be rising again as the academic job situation deteriorates.

Postdoctoral stipends for biomedical and behavioral scientists reported for 1976 (NRC, 1977, 2:131-2) showed considerable variation between the two areas; male postdoctorals in biomedical sciences earned 3.6 percent more

TABLE 3.6   Trends in Postdoctoral Stipends for Doctoral Scientists and Engineers by Sex, 1973-1977

	Median Annual Stipend[+]					
	1973		1975		1977	
	Men	Women	Men	Women	Men	Women
Number of Individuals[*]	2,427	588	5,137	1,254	6,173	1,572
Median Stipend	$8,760	$8,290	$10,980	$10,440	$12,180	$11,330
$ Difference in Medians	$470		$540		$850	
% Men's Stipends Exceed Women's	5.7%		4.9%		7.5%	

*The figures do not include individuals who earned doctorates in the last 6 months of the year preceding the survey year.

[+]Stipends for 9-10 months have been adjusted to a full-year equivalent.

Source: Survey of Doctorate Recipients, National Research Council

than women, but for behavioral scientists the men's earnings exceeded the women's by 11.8 percent. For postdoctorals under age 30, the differences were 1 percent and 6.5 percent for biomedical and behavioral scientists, respectively, but for those aged 30-39, men's earnings exceeded women's by 4.6 and 11.8 percent. When the data were controlled by marital status and sex (Table 4.21), married men were found to have the highest stipends.

Efforts to disaggregate the salary data for postdoctorals by field, Ph.D. cohort, and type of institution are not very informative because the various categories contain too few women to yield meaningful information.

Conclusions and Recommendations

A postdoctoral appointment is an important career stage intended as a springboard, but it is not clear that it yields the same results for women as for men. The responsibility for achieving maximal benefits from postdoctoral appointments rests individually with postdoctoral sponsors and collectively with science departments, and must be shared by women scientists themselves in a heightened awareness that decisions made at this career stage may have very far-reaching consequences.

Postdoctoral awards represent a gray area in equal opportunity, not explicitly addressed by the statutes referring to either education or employment. Depending on individual institutional practice, a postdoctoral may have student or staff status, or no defined status at all. For affirmative action monitoring, the position may therefore not be subject to reporting, or may fall in one of several possible categories, faculty among them. From the point of view of compliance (in addition to others, such as fair employment practices) clarification of postdoctoral status is needed.

Dependent as most postdoctoral awards are on federal research support, they comprise a category of employment which should be subject to more careful assessment of equality of opportunity. Research awards which support postdoctorals should ideally be contingent in part on effective provision of equal opportunity and demonstrable absence of biased procedures. Nonetheless, we hesitate to recommend a blanket policy of compliance monitoring of postdoctoral positions, mindful of the fact that agency program staffs are unlikely to be good compliance officers, and vice versa. As a beginning, however, major granting agencies, including especially NSF and NIH, should develop standards for effectively evaluating the bias-free distribution of postdoctoral appointments and methods for applying such standards to the award process. In order to provide a sound basis for such standards, the relationships between merit, nature, quality and number of awards, and sex, of the sort suggested in this report, need to be developed in greater detail. Investigators applying for postdoctoral funding could then evaluate their own progress, and would submit appropriate reports with their applications for support.

Such a procedure would have the advantage that responsibility and authority would rest with both individual departments and the specific persons most likely to be directly affected. By contrast, current regulations leave at least as great a paperwork burden on departments but ultimately spread the blame--and, if one were imposed, the penalty--over entire institutions.

On the basis of available data, it appears likely that at least a large part of the salary differences between men and women postdoctorals derives from bias. At this level no significant differences in overall ability or promise can be documented (see Chapter 2), and male and female scientists should be rewarded equally for comparable work. Systematic salary differences at this early career stage are important not only for their immediate relevance to equity but also as a portent of future status.

The case of sex differences in postdoctoral stipends presents difficult policy questions, however. In our judgment, individual stipends are apt to be determined more often by what the research budget will bear than by a prior decision to offer lower salaries to women as a group. Women who do not consider themselves primary wage earners or who lack alternatives may accept low offers more readily than men. Some of the differential we see in the data may be due to dependents' allowances provided in many kinds of fellowships; past experience suggests that women may not claim such allowances if they have employed husbands, or may not be granted them in such cases. We urge that the Commission on Human Resources study of postdoctoral staff currently in progress particularly address the details of these salary differentials. We believe salaries to be important indicators of possible discrimination as well as potential success. A detailed analysis, however, is outside the scope of the present study.

CHAPTER 4

ACADEMIC EMPLOYMENT

The Employment Patterns of Women Scientists

In this chapter we will be concerned with recent trends in the employment of women scientists as faculty members with particular attention to the rank of assistant professor where major new developments would be expected to occur first. Since research universities rarely appointed women to their science faculties in the past, we do not yet expect to find many women in their senior faculties. If equal opportunity policies are observed, we do expect to find women proportionally represented among newly hired junior faculty members, and we expect to find them being paid and promoted at the same rate as men.

As shown in Table 4.1, women doctoral scientists are less likely than men to be employed in industry and are more heavily represented in higher education. Within higher education, they are more likely to teach than men (Table 4.2). They are also far more likely than men to be found in the lower ranks; roughly two-thirds of male faculty are associate or full professors while only one-third of women faculty are at that rank. The distribution of women faculty is more skewed in the top institutions (by R&D expenditures) than in the others (Table 4.3 and Figure 4.1).

Our main concern in this section is to assess changes over the last few years in the traditional pattern. Because the proportions of women faculty vary widely among fields and their numbers are extremely small in some disciplines, any generalized analysis is of dubious utility. Set against the backdrop of a nearly steady-state academic economy and a sharply declining one in some fields, even a slight relative improvement in the status of women on science faculties can be regarded as a very welcome sign of progress.

TABLE 4.1   Percent of Employed* Doctoral Scientists and Engineers
             by Employment Sector and Sex, 1977

Number Employed	Total 267,206	Men 242,913	Women 24,293
Educational Institutions	56.2%	55.1	67.4%
4-Year Colleges/Univ.	53.9	53.2	61.3
2-Year Colleges	1.6	1.4	3.5
Elem/Secnd Schools	0.6	0.5	2.5
Business & Industry	26.4	27.9	11.6
Federal Government	8.4	8.8	4.9
Other Government	1.9	1.8	3.2
Hospitals & Clinics	2.9	2.5	7.3
Nonprofit Organizations	2.9	2.8	4.0
Other Employers	0.8	0.7	1.0
Employer Not Reported	0.5	0.4	0.7

* Excludes postdoctoral appointees.

Source: Survey of Doctorate Recipients, National Research Council.
          The statistics in this table are weighted estimates, derived
          from a sample survey of 65,000 Ph.D's in science and engineering.
          The estimates are subject to two types of error -- sampling and
          non-sampling, (e.g., non-response bias). A discussion of the
          survey is provided in Appendix D.

TABLE 4.2   Employment Sector and Primary Work Activity of Employed Doctoral
Scientists and Engineers, Excluding Postdoctoral Appointees,
by Sex, 1973-1977

	Total		Men		Women	
	1973	1977	1973	1977	1973	1977
All Sectors & Activities	209,808	267,206	194,506	242,913	15,302	24,293
Educational Inst.	57.8%	56.2%	56.8%	55.1%	71.4%	67.4%
Research	12.6	13.1	12.5	13.1	15.1	13.9
Teaching	36.4	32.2	35.7	31.4	45.8	39.9
Administration	6.2	7.2	6.2	7.3	5.4	6.6
Other	2.6	3.7	2.4	3.3	5.1	7.0
Federal Government	9.3	8.4	9.5	8.8	6.0	4.9
Research	4.8	4.0	4.9	4.2	3.0	2.5
Administration	3.4	3.2	3.6	3.4	1.5	1.5
Other	1.1	1.2	1.1	1.2	1.4	1.0
Business & Industry	25.2	26.4	26.5	27.9	8.4	11.6
Research	11.2	11.7	11.9	12.5	3.0	3.7
Administration	9.4	8.9	10.0	9.7	1.1	1.4
All Other	4.5	5.8	4.6	5.7	4.3	6.5
All Other Employers	7.7	9.0	7.2	8.3	14.2	16.1
Research	2.8	2.7	2.7	2.6	4.0	3.7
Administration	2.5	2.7	2.5	2.6	3.0	3.7
All Other	2.4	3.6	2.1	3.0	7.2	8.7

Source: Survey of Doctorate Recipients, National Research Council.
The statistics in this table are weighted estimates, derived from a
sample survey of 65,000 Ph.D.'s in science and engineering. The
estimates are subject to two types of error, sampling and non-sampling,
(e.g., nonresponse bias). A discussion of the survey is provided in
Appendix D.

TABLE 4.3   Percent Distribution of Doctoral Scientists and Engineers in Academe*
by Faculty Rank, R&D Expenditures of Employment Institution+, and
Sex, 1977

	Top 25 Inst. by R&D		Second 25 Inst. by R&D		Other Institutions	
	Men	Women	Men	Women	Men	Women
No. Employed, incl Postdocs.	17,664	1,979	14,116	1,384	92,155	12,392
Professor	44.7%	9.8%	42.4%	13.4%	37.0%	16.0%
Assoc. Prof.	19.5	14.6	24.7	18.4	30.3	24.3
Asst. Prof.	15.0	31.0	20.0	36.0	23.4	38.4
Inst./Lect.	0.9	6.8	1.4	4.9	2.0	5.7
Other/No Report	9.5	18.2	5.4	12.8	3.7	7.9
Postdocs.	10.4	19.6	6.1	14.5	3.5	7.7

* Includedare two-year and four-year colleges, universities, and medical schools.

+ See Appendix B-1 for a description of the ranking of institutions by
federal R&D expenditures.

NOTE: Percents may not add to 100.0% due to rounding.

Source: Survey of Doctorate Recipients, National Research Council.
The statistics in this table are weighted estimates, derived
from a sample survey of 65,000 Ph.D's in science and engineering.
The estimates are subject to two types of error -- sampling and
non-sampling, (e.g., non-response bias). A discussion of the
survey is provided in Appendix D.

FIGURE 4.1   Faculty Rank Distribution of Doctoral Scientists and Engineers by
R&D Expenditures of Institution* and Sex, 1977.

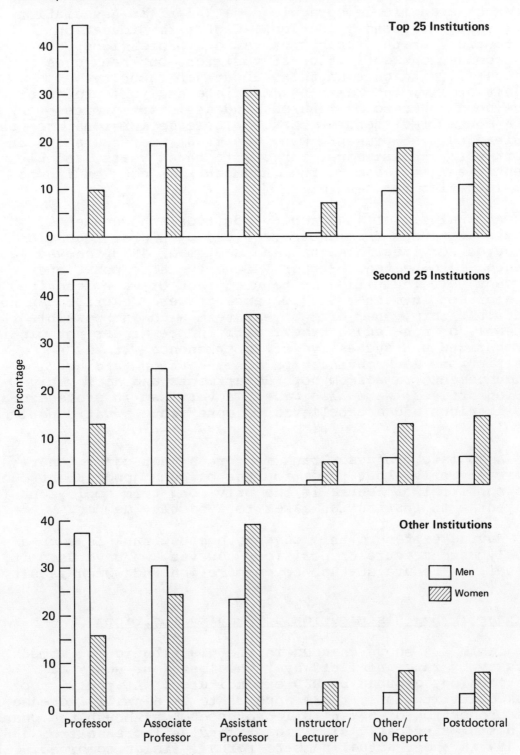

*See Appendix B-1 for a description of the ranking of institutions by federal R&D expenditures.

SOURCE: Survey of Doctorate Recipients, National Research Council.

Rank vs. Tenure as Definitions of Position

Most academic demographic data (American Association of University Professors, National Center for Education Statistics, status reports on various professions) use rank as a convenient definition of position, but rank does not necessarily indicate anything about job security. Traditionally, the ranks of associate and full professor have been taken to be tenured, and assistant professorships were considered "tenure-track." These definitions are now misleading. At present, many assistant professorships are short-term appointments, for one to three years, and clearly identified (at least to the incumbent) as not leading to consideration for tenure.

An analysis of 164 faculty position announcements, chosen at random from those received by Higher Education Resource Services in August and September 1978, showed less than half to be tenure-track. Seventy-three positions or 45 percent were identified as tenure-track or were described as "senior appointment"; 52 (32 percent) were described as non-renewable term, one- or two-year term with one possible renewal, or non-tenure track, with the remainder not clearly categorized but suggestive of impermanence with such descriptions as "continuation contingent on funding." Announcements came from both departments and affirmative action offices, were also widely advertised in professional publications and are believed to constitute a valid national sample.

Associate professor rank may or may not carry tenure; typically only about three fourths of such appointments do. The conferral of tenure is the only long-term employment guarantee an institution makes to a faculty member.

Having expressed this caveat, because rank is such a widely used measure of position, however, we have used it, as well as tenure status, to compare men and women faculty.

Changes in Sex Distribution of Faculty Positions

Table 4.4 shows changes in the distribution of women faculty by rank and field over the last four years at institutions grouped by R&D expenditures. At the 25 top-ranked institutions, there appears to be a small increase in the proportion of women full professors, although the change is not statistically significant, and an increase from 138 to 194 in their actual numbers for all fields combined. The increases in the life sciences are positive, and may represent an upgrading of in-house candidates. In engineering, mathematics, and physical sciences (EMP fields), women were only one percent of the full professors in 1977, despite an apparent increase in their numbers. At the associate level, the estimated proportions of women show an increase from 6 to 8 percent across all science fields, although due to small numbers, this is not statistically significant. At the assistant level, though, the trend was clearly up.

The second 25 institutions displayed a similar pattern, with however a statistically significant overall increase at the full professor rank, due to appointments of women in the life sciences. At assistant rank, the proportions again notably increased between 1973 and 1977.

The "other" institutions displayed no overall growth in the percentages of women among full professors, although women are still more highly represented here than in the top 50 institutions. There was a marked increase in the proportions of women among assistant professors. Overall, in 1977 the picture was one of higher proportions of women senior faculty at the "other" institutions, with some gains, however, being made at the first 50.

In the sciences as a group, there has been moderate growth with total faculty positions (assistant professor rank and above) increasing by 21.5 percent in four years, from 1973 to 1977, for an average growth rate of 5.4 percent per year (Table 4.5). When institutions are grouped by R&D expenditures, however, only 5.5 percent of the total growth has occurred in the top 25 institutions, 2.9 percent in the second 25, and 91.6 percent in all others. Women account for 21.3 percent of the overall increase in faculty positions, a slightly higher figure than their average share of recent doctorates (see Table 2.1). Women on science faculties increased about three times faster than total faculty growth between 1973 and 1977. The more detailed dimensions and the uneven character of the "academic depression" are summarized in Tables 4.5 and 4.6.

In the top 25 universities, nearly 70 percent of the entire faculty increase is in the social sciences; mathematics, medical sciences, and biosciences have all declined substantially in this group (Table 4.6). Within the EMP fields there are notable differences which deserve comment. Table 4.6 indicates that, in the top 25 institutions, the proportions of women on mathematics, physics, and chemistry faculties have not changed materially, whereas departments of earth sciences and engineering in this top category have made four-fold increases; however, because of the small numbers of women faculty then and now in the EMP fields, the differences are not statistically significant.

If we examine engineering, mathematics, and the physical sciences at institutions of differing rank, as in Table 4.7, we note a lower-than-average growth rate in all

TABLE 4.4a   Number and Percent of Women Doctoral Scientists and Engineers in Faculty Positions, by R & D Expenditures of Institution, Field, and Sex, 1973 and 1977.

Top 25 Institutions

	Professor		Associate		Assistant	
	1973	1977	1973	1977	1973	1977
All Science/Eng. Flds.						
Total No.	7,460	8,085	3,464	3,741	3,206	3,264
No. Women	138	194	205	289	368	614
% Women	1.8	2.4	5.9	7.7	11.5	18.8
	(+0.4)	(+0.5)	(+1.0)	(+1.2)	(+2.9)	(+2.0)
Engr.,Math,Phys.Sc.						
Total No.	3,104	3,671	1,426	1,439	1,170	1,141
No. Women	22	28	12	29	50	92
% Women	0.7	0.8	0.8	2.0	4.3	8.1
	(+0.4)	(+0.4)	(+0.6)	(+1.1)	(+1.6)	(+2.3)
Life Sciences						
Total No.	2,295	2,089	1,180	1,196	1,105	868
No. Women	50	88	100	104	153	216
% Women	2.2	4.2	8.5	8.7	13.8	24.9
	(+0.7)	(+1.1)	(+1.9)	(+2.1)	(+2.4)	(+3.9)
Behav. & Social Sc.						
Total No.	2,061	2,325	858	1,106	931	1,255
No. Women	66	78	93	156	165	306
% Women	3.2	3.4	10.8	14.1	17.7	24.4
	(+1.1)	(+1.1)	(+2.7)	(+3.0)	(+3.4)	(+3.8)

*See appendix B-1 for a description of ranking of institutions by federal R&D expenditures.

Note: Estimated sampling errors associated with the percent statistics are shown in parentheses.

Source: Survey of Doctorate Recipients, National Research Council. The statistics in this table are weighted estimates derived from a sample survey of 65,000 Ph.D's in science and engineering. The estimates are subject to two types of error -- sampling and non-sampling, (e.g., nonresponse bias). A discussion of the survey is provided in Appendix D.

TABLE 4.4b   Number and Percent of Women Doctoral Scientists and
              Engineers in Faculty Positions, by R & D Expenditures of
              Institution, Field, and Sex, 1973 and 1977.

<u>Second 25 Institutions</u>

	Professor		Associate		Assistant	
	1973	1977	1973	1977	1973	1977
All Science/Eng.Flds.						
Total No.	5,919	6,168	3,681	3,746	3,122	3,319
No. Women	102	185	199	255	265	498
% Women	1.7	3.0	5.4	6.8	8.5	15.0
	(+0.4)	(+0.6)	(+0.9)	(+1.2)	(+1.3)	(+1.8)
Engr., Math, Phys. Sc.						
Total No.	2,479	2,772	1,494	1,478	1,509	1,190
No. Women	13	27	21	23	52	79
% Women	0.5	1.0	1.4	1.6	3.4	6.6
	(+0.4)	(+0.5)	(+0.8)	(+1.0)	(+1.3)	(+2.1)
Life Sciences						
Total No.	2,177	1,975	1,320	1,238	988	1,152
No. Women	37	87	83	110	103	135
% Women	1.7	4.4	6.3	8.9	10.4	11.7
	(+0.7)	(+1.2)	(+1.6)	(+2.2)	(+2.3)	(+2.6)
Behav. & Social Sc						
Total No.	1,263	1,415	867	1,030	625	977
No. Women	52	71	95	122	110	284
% Women	4.1	5.0	11.0	11.8	17.6	29.1
	(+1.6)	(+1.7)	(+2.8)	(+3.1)	(+4.1)	(+4.3)

*See Appendix B-1 for a description of ranking of institutions by federal R&D expenditures.

Note: Estimated sampling errors associated with the percent statistics are shown in
      parentheses.

Source: Survey of Doctorate Recipients, National Research Council. The statistics in
        this table are weighted estimates derived from a sample survey of 65,000 Ph. D's
        in science and engineering. The estimates are subject to two types of error --
        sampling and non-sampling, (e.g., nonresponse bias). A discussion of the survey
        is provided in Appendix D.

TABLE 4.4c   Number and Percent of Women Doctoral Scientists and
              Engineers in Faculty Positions, by R & D Expenditures of
              Institution, Field, and Sex, 1973 and 1977.

<u>Other Institutions</u>

	Professor		Associate		Assistant	
	1973	1977	1973	1977	1973	1977
All Science/Eng. Flds						
Total No.	28,610	36,103	23,930	30,927	21,789	26,325
No. Women	1,563	1,988	1,868	3,013	2,714	4,759
% Women	5.5	5.5	7.8	9.7	12.5	18.1
	(+0.3)	(+0.3)	(+0.4)	(+0.5)	(+0.6)	(+0.7)
Engr., Math, Phys. Sc						
Total No.	11,517	14,923	10,045	12,303	8,383	8,397
No. Women	338	429	386	516	468	733
% Women	2.9	2.9	3.8	4.2	5.6	8.7
	(+0.4)	(+0.4)	(+0.5)	(+0.5)	(+0.7)	(+0.9)
Life Sciences						
Total No.	8,877	10,984	6,909	8,865	6,375	8,346
No. Women	591	668	687	1,034	895	1,629
% Women	6.7	6.1	9.9	11.7	14.0	19.5
	(+0.6)	(+0.6)	(+0.9)	(+0.9)	(+1.1)	(+1.1)
Behav. & Social Sc						
Total No.	8,216	10,196	6,976	9,759	7,031	9,582
No. Women	634	891	795	1,463	1,351	2,397
% Women	7.7	8.7	11.4	15.0	19.2	25.0
	(+0.8)	(+0.8)	(+1.0)	(+1.1)	(+1.3)	(+1.4)

*See Appendix B-1 for a description of ranking of institutions by federal R&D expenditures.

Note: Estimated sampling errors associated with the percent statistics are shown in
      parentheses.

Source: Survey of Doctorate Recipients, National Research Council. The statistics in
        this table are weighted estimates derived from a sample survey of 65,000 Ph. D's
        in science and engineering. The estimates are subject to two types of error --
        sampling and non-sampling, (e.g., nonresponse bias). A discussion of the survey
        is provided in Appendix D.

TABLE 4.5   Increase in Doctoral Scientists and Engineers in Faculty*
            Positions by R&D Expenditures of Institution+ and Sex,
            1973-1977

		Total Science** Faculty	Number of Women	Women as % of 1973-1977 Increase
Total All Inst.++	1977	123,230	12,092	
	1973	101,405	7,437	
	4-Yr Growth	21,825 (21.5%)	4,655	21.3%
Total 1st 50 Inst.	1977	28,727	2,109	
	1973	26,894	1,277	
	4-Yr Growth	1,833 (6.8%)	832	45.4%
Top 25 Inst.	1977	15,352	1,129	
	1973	14,153	711	
	4-Yr Growth	1,199 (8.5%)	418	34.9%
Second 25 Inst.	1977	13,375	980	
	1973	12,741	566	
	4-Yr Growth	634 (5.0%)	414	65.3%
Other Inst.	1977	94,503	9,983	
	1973	74,511	6,160	
	4-Yr Growth	19,992 (26.8%)	3,823	19.1%

* Faculty includes professor, associate professor, and assistant professor ranks.

+ See Appedix B-1 for a description of ranking of institutions by federal R&D
  expenditures.

** Fields included are mathematics, computer sciences, physics/astronomy, chemistry,
   earth sciences, engineering, agricultural sciences, medical sciences, biological
   sciences, psychology, and social sciences.

++ Includes two-year and four-year colleges, universities, and medical schools.

Source: Survey of Doctorate Recipients, National Research Council.
          The statistics in this table are weighted estimates, derived
          from a sample survey of 65,000 Ph.D's in science and engineering.
          The statistics are subject to two types of error -- sampling and
          non-sampling, (e.g., non-response bias). A discussion of the sur-
          vey is provided in Appendix D.

67

TABLE 4.6 Increase in Doctoral Scientists and Engineers in Faculty* Positions at 25 Leading Institutions+ by Field and Sex, 1973-1977

	Men and Women		Women	
	1973 Faculty	Net Gain, 1973-1977	1973 Faculty	Net Gain, 1973-1977
Mathematics**	1,394	-219 (-16%)	42	[-10 (-24%)]
Physics /Astronomy	1,208	53 (4%)	20	[12 (60%)]
Chemistry	668	68 (10%)	11	[3 (27%)]
Earth Sciences	619	94 (15%)	6	27 (450%)
Engineering	1,811	393 (22%)	5	[20 (400%)]
Agricultural Sciences	822	221 (27%)	14	[9 (64%)]
Medical Sciences	806	-187 (-23%)	66	40 (61%)
Biological Sciences	2,967	-400 (-13%)	223	76 (34%)
Psychology	1,299	46 (4%)	154	85 (55%)
Social Sciences	2,559	834 (33%)	170	140 (82%)

*Faculty includes professor, associate professor, and assistant professor ranks.
+The top 25 institutions by R&D expenditures in FY 1976 are included. See Appendix B-1 for a listing of the institutions.
**The apparent decrease in mathematics faculty may be in part due to a redefinition of departments, separating applied mathematics, statistics, or computer sciences from pure mathematics.
[]Brackets indicate that the apparent net gain or loss between 1973 and 1977 is not statistically significant.

Source: Survey of Doctorate Recipients, National Research Council. The statistics in this table are weighted estimates, derived from a sample survey of 65,000 Ph.D's in science and engineering. The statistics are subject to two types of error -- sampling and non-sampling (e.g., non-response bias). A discussion of the survey is provided in Appendix D.

institutions, and a quite steady state in the top 50.
Compared to the previous two decades of rapid growth in
these departments, this is indeed a depression. Women have
fared a good deal better in these departments than men in
percentage gains, but they remain a very small proportion of
all faculty. In these 50 universities in all EMP fields
combined, there was a total of 261 women of faculty rank in
1977-- or an average of about one woman for every
department. In the remaining institutions (the great
majority of colleges and universities) the number of women
in EMP fields has increased by more than one-third, but,
again, because the total is small compared to male faculty,
their proportion of all faculty positions remains low.

The table also points up interesting differences in the
responses of various types of institutions to demands for
equal opportunity. The top 50 universities, because of
their high visibility and their very low proportion of women
faculty in the past, have been special targets in the
affirmative action debate. Because of their very large
share of federal R&D funds, some of them are also currently
targets of special pre-award compliance reviews.

To our knowledge, only a half dozen compliance reviews
have been conducted. An analysis of one case casts some
light on the character of the reviews and the possible
conclusions that may be drawn from them. In connection with
its recently completed compliance review, Harvard University
has published a comparison of projected and actual hiring
(Harvard Gazette, September 29, 1978), abstracted here in
Table 4.8. Internally established goals for women were not
met at tenured and ladder (tenure-track) ranks but were
slightly exceeded at "other instructional" ranks. It is
interesting to note that the much greater difficulty of
locating minority faculty than women faculty (in relation to
the Ph.D. pool of each) is only minimally reflected either
in Harvard's goals or actual appointments. In the Faculty
of Arts and Sciences, which had a total of 352 members in
1978, the goal for tenured minority faculty was 21, with 20
actually in place, compared to a goal of 14 women at which
time 12 held tenured positions. At ladder rank, there were
16 minority faculty members in 1978 in relation to a goal of
15, but 49 women as opposed to a projected 56. The tenure
distribution of minority faculty (20 tenured and 16 ladder)
resembles that of the total faculty (352 tenured and 220
ladder); for women the order is reversed at 12 tenured and
49 ladder. Of these 12 tenured women, two were in biology;
there were no tenured women faculty in any other science
department. The compliance review was favorable, and
Harvard will continue to receive public funding. It is
important to note that, as a rule, science departments are
the major beneficiaries of federal funds in universities,
and are therefore especially vulnerable to possible loss of
such funds.

Table 4.7   Changes in Size and Sex Composition of Doctoral Faculty* in
             EMP** Fields by R&D Expenditures of Institution+, 1973-1977

		Total Faculty	Women Faculty	
			Number	%
Top 25 Institutions	1977	6,089	136	2.2%
	1973	5,700	84	1.5
4-yr. Growth		389	52	
%		+6.8%	+62.0%	
Second 25 Institutions	1977	5,399	125	2.3
	1973	5,490	86	1.6
4-yr. Growth		-191	39	
		-3.5%	+45.0%	
Other Institutions	1977	34,740	1,642	4.7
	1973	30,008	1,192	4.0
4-yr. Growth		4,732	450	
		+15.8%	+37.8%	

*Faculty includes full professors, associate professors, and assistant professors at two-year and four-year colleges, universities, and medical schools.

+See Appendix B-1 for a description of ranking of institutions by R&D expenditures.

**EMP fields are mathematics, physics/astronomy, chemistry, earth sciences, and engineering. Computer sciences are omitted because they were not reported separately for 1973.

Source: Survey of Doctorate Recipients, National Research Council. The statistics in this table are weighted estimates, derived from a sample survey of 65,000 Ph.D.'s in science and engineering. The statistics are subject to two types of error -- sampling and non-sampling, (e.g., non-response bias). A discussion of the survey is provided in Appendix B.

TABLE 4.8   Affirmative Action Faculty Statistics, Past and Present

Faculty of Arts and Sciences

Harvard University

	Total	Minorities	Women
Tenured Faculty			
7/72	361	15	6
(Projected 6/76)	*(386)*	*(17)*	*(12)*
12/76	372	19	12
(Projected 6/78)	*(395)*	*(21)*	*(14)*
6/78	352	20	12
Ladder Rank			
7/73	194	10	21
(Projected 6/76)	*(229)*	*(18)*	*(37)*
12/76	214	15	47
(Projected 6/78)	*(228)*	*(15)*	*(56)*
6/78	220	16	49
Other Instructional			
7/73	144	21	37
(Projected 6/76)	*(121)*	*(18)*	*(36)*
12/76	98	22	37
(Projected 6/78)	*(89)*	*(22)*	*(28)*
6/78	75	16	36

NOTE: 6/76 projections from 1973 Affirmative Action Plan.
6/78 projections from 1976 Affirmative Action Plan

Source: Harvard Gazette, September 29, 1978.

In any case, in terms of recent improvement, the record of the top 50 universities is better than that of the vastly larger group of "other" institutions, which employ about three times as many people although they spend a great deal less federal money.

Given the difficulty of identifying trends from such small numbers, and bearing in mind that within the "top 25" category we are looking at 25 different departments in each field which all have their own more or less unique problems of age, rank, and specialty distributions, it is possible to draw some conclusions regarding employment of women by these faculties. Chemistry departments remain almost entirely male and show no significant change. In mathematics there is also no significant change, apparently due to the decrease in total positions; however, the fields of medical sciences and biological sciences experienced comparable declines in total positions, yet increased their numbers of women faculty during the same period. Chemistry and mathematics have consistently produced many more women doctorates than other EMP areas (Table 2.1). The proportion of women faculty at the top 25 institutions in either field has not exceeded three percent, although women were six and seven percent of the doctoral labor force. The disparities between supply and utilization are much larger than in the other science fields. In earth sciences and engineering, both producing few women doctorates until very recently, they are well represented, in relation to availability.

In the remaining science fields--biological, medical, and social sciences (Tables 4.9 and 4.10)--the proportions of women on faculties have traditionally been higher than in the EMP fields although here, too, they were considerably below their representation in the doctoral labor force (Table 2.8). Agricultural sciences remain an exception in this group, with a history very similar to that of chemistry of near-total prior exclusion of women faculty, but better results in catching up. In all of these fields, involving much larger total numbers of faculty, women have made strong gains. Even in medical sciences in the top institutional category and in biosciences in both upper groups, where substantial cuts were made in total faculty between 1973 and 1977, appointments of women increased significantly.

An additional element to be considered in hiring is illustrated in Table 4.11 which shows the extent to which leading departments in six fields hire their own and each other's Ph.D's. The fields are selected to illustrate a range in the degree to which the disciplines are experimental in nature since this property is correlated with fractions of postdoctoral and off-ladder appointments by field. For the departments shown in Table 4.11, the percentages of men and women hired who are their own (or comparable) graduates are quite similar, except for

72

TABLE 4.9   Changes in Size and Sex Composition of Doctoral Faculty* in
             the Life Sciences,by R&D Expenditures of Institution+,
             1973-1977

| | | Total Faculty | Women Faculty | |
			Number	%
Top 25 Inst.	1977	4,229	428	10.1%
	1973	4,595	303	6.6
	4-Yr Growth	-366	125	
	%	-8.0%	41.3%	
Second 25 Inst.	1977	4,389	348	7.9
	1973	4,496	223	5.0
	4-Yr Growth	-107	125	
	%	-2.4%	56.1%	
Other Inst.	1977	28,521	3,399	11.9
	1973	22,200	2,173	9.8
	4-Yr Growth	6,321	1,226	
	%	28.5%	56.4%	

* Faculty includes full-professors, associate professors, and assistant profes-
   sors at two-year and four-year colleges, universities, and medical schools.
+ See Appendix B-1 for a description of ranking of institutions by federal
   R&D expenditures.

Source: Survey of Doctorate Recipients, National Research Council.
          The statistics in this table are weighted estimates, derived from
          a sample survey of 65,000 Ph. D's in science and engineering. The
          estimates are subject to two types of error - sampling and non-sampling,
          (e.g., non-response bias). A discussion of the survey is provided in
          Appendix D.

TABLE 4.10 Changes in Size and Sex Composition of Doctoral Faculty* in
Psychology and Social Sciences,by R&D Expenditures of
Institutions+, 1973-1977

		Total Faculty	Women Faculty	
			Number	%
Top 25 Inst.	1977	4,738	549	11.6%
	1973	3,858	324	8.4
	4-Yr Growth	880	225	
	%	22.8%	69.4%	
Second 25 Inst.	1977	3,447	496	14.4
	1973	2,755	257	9.3
	4-Yr Growth	692	239	
	%	25.1%	93.0%	
Other Inst.	1977	29,993	4,881	16.3
	1973	22,303	2,795	12.5
	4-Yr Growth	7,690	2,086	
	%	34.5%	74.6%	

* Faculty includes full professors, associate professors, and
  assistant professors at two-year and four-year colleges,
  universities, and medical schools.
+ See Appendix B-1 for a description of ranking of institutions
  by federal R&D expenditures.

Source: Survey of Doctorate Recipeints, National Research Council.
The statistics in this table are weighted estimates, derived
from a sample survey of 65,000 Ph.D.'s in science and
engineering. The estimates are subject to two types of
error - sampling and non-sampling, (e.g., non-response bias).
A discussion of the survey is provided in Appendix D.

TABLE 4.11   Employment of Ph.D.'s from Highly-Rated Departments* in Six Science Fields by Sex, 1977

	Physics/Astronomy		Math/Computer		Chemistry		Microbiology		Psychology		Sociology	
	Men	Women	Men	Women	Men	Women	Men	Women	Men	Women	Men	Women
Ph.D.'s from Leading Departments Who Were Employed+ in Academe in 1977 - Total	6,904	189	5,192	426	7,497	657	1,191	335	5,919	1,753	2,152	564
Employed in Other Than Highly-Rated Depts. (%)	68.1%	63.5%	72.8%	82.9%	78.9%	78.1%	81.2%	76.7%	76.8%	76.1%	79.9%	81.4%
Employed in Highly-Rated Departments												
Faculty (%)	16.8	14.3	23.2	12.0	13.4	4.0	10.9	7.2	18.6	15.8	16.7	16.1
Non-Faculty (%)	15.0	22.2	4.0	5.2	7.7	18.0	7.9	16.1	4.6	8.1	3.4	2.5

*Roose-Andersen rating. For an explanation of the rating and the lists of the highly-rated institutions in each field, see Appendix B-2.

+Includes those employed full-time and part-time, and postdoctoral appointees.

**Faculty includes professors, associate professors, and assistant professors.

Source: Survey of Doctorate Recipients, National Research Council. The statistics in this table are weighted estimates, derived from a sample survey of 65,000 Ph.D.'s in science and engineering. The estimates are subject to two types of error - sampling and non-sampling (e.g., nonresponse bias). A discussion of the survey is provided in Appendix D.

mathematics; however, the percentages hired as faculty are markedly different, varying with the availability of off-ladder positions. Table 4.12 shows that in those fields where the option of off-ladder or research appointments is open, women are hired preferentially in non-faculty positions. Where this option does not exist, women become faculty members if they are hired at all. Table 4.13 shows that the predominance of women over men at the instructor/lecturer rank increased at the top 25 institutions from 1973 to 1977, remained the same at the second 25, and decreased only at the "other" institutions.

Off-Ladder Positions

As a general rule, departments hire professional staff in variously designated positions which are outside the tenure stream. Such positions may be a holding pattern for people they would like to keep until a more promising appointment becomes available. More frequently, however, they are marginal jobs, fluctuating with enrollments, unexpected leaves of regular faculty, and other exigencies. Some are used as semi-permanent ways to teach service courses or supervise laboratory instruction. Many such positions are part-time or part-year, often obviating the need to pay even prorated benefits. They provide a very economical way for science departments to get the chores done. In virtually all the cases with which we are familiar, people in such off-ladder positions are not permitted to apply for outside research support, thus eliminating any chances they might have to establish independent research records and improve their prospects. Women are heavily over-represented in positions of this sort. The considerable fluctuations over time and among fields with otherwise similar characteristics that are apparent in Table 4.12 testify to the marginal nature of this academic labor supply.

Persons characterized as "instructor/lecturer" and "other/no report" are not included in faculty ranks but are departmental employees; postdoctoral appointments also fall into this category but have already been discussed in Chapter 3, so that the data under consideration here concern only the first two classifications. Table 4.14 shows the numbers and percentages of women, for all science fields, who held such off-ladder positions in 1973 and 1977. Not only the absolute numbers but the proportions of women in off-ladder positions increased between 1973 and 1977 in all except two categories ("other/no report" in the top 25 institutions and "instuctor/lecturer" in the "other" institutions). It should be noted, however, that the total numbers of both men and women in off-ladder positions are small compared to total faculty.

TABLE 4.12 Number and Percent of Doctoral Scientists and Engineers
in Academe* at Rank of Instructor/Lecturer, by Field and
Sex, 1973-1977

| Field | 1973 | | | | 1977 | | | |
| | Men | | Women | | Men | | Women | |
	No.	%	No.	%	No.	%	No.	%
Mathematics	125	1.2	48	7.5	833	8.2	90	10.9
Physics/Astronomy	173	2.5	26	9.6	173	1.9	35	12.4
Chemistry	222	2.3	92	11.9	264	2.3	100	8.4
Earth Sciences	23	0.5	8	5.3	38	0.7	9	3.6
Engineering	41	0.3	**	4.0	154	1.1	**	5.0
Agricultural Sci.	25	0.4	**	**	57	0.7	4	2.8
Medical Sci.	122	2.6	32	5.1	169	2.5	59	5.0
Biological Sci.	338	1.6	174	5.2	443	1.8	267	5.5
Psychology	81	0.4	125	6.4	228	2.0	162	5.2
Social Sciences	153	0.9	82	4.1	341	1.5	176	4.7

*Included are two-year and four-year colleges, universities, and medical
 schools.
**Estimates based on fewer than three sample individuals are not shown.

  Source: Survey of Doctorate ecipients, National Research Council.

TABLE 4.13 Number and Percent of Doctoral Scientists and Engineers in
Academe* at Rank of Instructor/Lecturer, by R&D Expenditures
of Employment Institution[+] and Sex, 1973-1977

| R&D Expenditures of Employment Institution | 1973 | | | | 1977 | | | |
| | Men | | Women | | Men | | Women | |
	No.	%	No.	%	No.	%	No.	%
Top 25 Institutions	217	1.3	81	5.9	154	0.9	134	6.8
Second 25 Institutions	151	1.1	38	4.6	192	1.4	68	4.9
Other Institutions	935	1.3	470	6.1	1,877	2.0	704	5.7

*Included are two-year and four-year colleges, universities, and medical schools.
+See Appendix B-1 for a description of the ranking of institutions by R&D
 expenditures
**Estimates based on fewer than three sample individuals are not shown.

  Source: Survey of Doctorate Recipients, National Research Council.

TABLE 4.14 Number and Percent of Women Doctoral Scientists and Engineers in Selected Positions in Academic Institutions[*] by R&D Expenditures of Institution[+], 1973-1977

| | 1973 | | 1977 | |
	No.	%	No.	%
Top 25 Institutions				
Total Employed in Academe	1370	7.6	1979	10.1
Faculty**	711	5.0	1129	7.4
Instr./Lectr.	81	27.2	134	46.5
Postdoctorals	209	11.7	387	17.4
Other/Rank Not Reported	369	21.5	329	18.5
Second 25 Institutions				
Total Employed in Academe	825	5.7	1384	8.9
Faculty	566	4.4	980	7.3
Instr./Lectr.	38	20.1	68	26.2
Postdoctorals	124	14.1	200	18.9
Other/Rank Not Reported	97	14.0	136	16.9
Other Institutions				
Total Employed in Academe	7643	9.4	12392	11.9
Faculty	6160	8.3	9983	10.6
Instr./Lectr.	470	33.5	704	27.3
Postdoctorals	443	17.6	951	22.5
Other/Rank Not Reported	570	22.5	754	23.3

[*]Includes two-year and four-year colleges, universities, and medical schools.
[+]See Appendix B-1 for a description of ranking of institutions by R&D expenditures.
**Includes full professors, associate professors, and assistant professors.

Source: Survey of Doctorate Recipients, National Research Council. The statistics in this table are weighted estimates, derived from a sample survey of 65,000 Ph.D.'s in science and engineering. The statistics are subject to two types of error -- sampling and non-sampling (e.g., non-response bias). A discussion of the survey is provided in Appendix B.

Positions of this sort do at least provide some employment for women (and a much smaller fraction of men) who cannot find more promising appointments. Traditionally they have been viewed as opportunities to continue some professional activity for women scientists who were ineligible for regular positions because of nepotism rules or overt sex bias, or who temporarily preferred less demanding commitments for personal reasons. If positions of this type were restructured to encourage some individual initiatives, access to research facilities and funding, and broader professional contacts, their impact on women scientists would be a good deal less detrimental. Programs to further such professional development for people in off-ladder positions need not be costly; in many cases they would involve changes in attitudes and institutional policies rather than expenditures. However, a modest funding program to provide for research costs, including overhead, would encourage more rapid changes in attitudes. The National Science Foundation's Women in Science program would be an appropriate location for such a project, perhaps on an experimental basis.

Promotion and Tenure

Whether or not women faculty are promoted to the upper ranks and to tenure—the two are not necessarily equivalent—provides a particularly sensitive test of the commitment of universities to equality of opportunity. A great many charges have been levelled at academic institutions in the past few years concerning their readiness to give women "revolving-door" appointments—short-term assistant professorships with no prospects of consideration for tenure and therefore none of the security necessary to become established and to initiate and carry out research. Reports of studies in progress at several major research universities have indicated internal concern that the rates of promotion to tenure for female junior faculty are well below those for men.[1]

Simple counting of positions by rank and sex (Table 4.15) does not lend support to such charges. Women have indeed done very well as a proportion of new hires, i.e. assistant professors, although the available pool is not being drained. Their rate of increase at this rank suggests that some women who have held long-term postdoctoral or other off-ladder positions are being appointed to faculty posts. This inference is supported by numerous case histories.[2] The increases at associate and full professor ranks represent promotions and presumably include some inter-institutional movement which may or may not differ systematically for the two sexes. Again, women seem to be doing well in promotions, especially in the top 50 institutions where, however, their actual numbers are very small. In the more numerous "other institution" category, they are advancing much less rapidly perhaps in part due to a transfer of the best women at these institutions to the more prestigious ones. Still, at the associate professor level they are advancing in proportions comparable to their presence as assistant professors.

These data tell us little that might resolve the "revolving door" or flow-through problem. Promotions made between 1973 and 1977 went to individuals who had been hired about 1970, on the average, with occasional exceptions for "fast track" individuals. Monitoring comparative rates of promotion for male and female assistant professors over the next five to seven years will shed some light on the problem but will not give conclusive answers. People who have held only short-term appointments in top universities may move down to similar posts in lower-ranking institutions, perhaps displacing individuals who leave the system altogether. Various other permutations are possible, but eventually many such people become ineligible for further academic positions through length of prior service, or they are simply viewed as undesirable through having been terminated too often, for whatever reason. Whether this is happening disproportionately often to women is a question that should be investigated now by longitudinal studies. It is possible, however, that salary analyses may illuminate this problem to some extent. This possibility is discussed below (p. 97).

Before presenting data comparing men and women with respect to tenure, it should be pointed out that an additional factor needs to be considered. This is indicated by a recent tabulation by marital status of the tenure standing of 1971-1975 Ph.D.'s in the biomedical and behavioral sciences who were employed in academic institutions in 1976 (NRC, 1977, Vol. 2, p. 138). The results showed that in both fields, married women were somewhat less likely than single men or women to hold tenured or tenure-track positions, but the differences were small. Large differences were noted, however, between these three groups and married men who were far more likely to hold such appointments. Thus, 65 percent of the married men in the biological sciences held tenured or tenure-track positions (compared with 43 percent of the unmarried men, 38 percent of the married women and 44 percent of the single women). In the behavioral sciences, 83 percent of the married men were in tenured or tenure-track appointments (as opposed to 70 percent of the single men, 69 percent of the married women, and 72 percent of the single women). In this respect again, married men present the picture of high achievers. It should be recalled that married men make up more than half of all Ph.D. recipients.

TABLE 4.15   Changes in Doctoral Science and Engineering Faculty by Rank, R&D
Expenditures of Employment Institution*, and Sex, 1973-1977

Top 25 Institutions

| | Professor | | | Assoc. Professor | | | Asst. Professor | | |
	Men	Women (%)		Men	Women (%)		Men	Women (%)
1977	7891	194 (2.5%)		3452	289 (8.4%)		2650	614 (23.2%)
1973	7322	138 (1.9%)		3259	205 (6.3%)		2838	368 (13.0%)
4-Yr Growth	569	56		193	84		-188	+246
Women as % of total increase		9.8%			30%			100%

Second 25 Institutions

	Men	Women (%)		Men	Women (%)		Men	Women (%)
1977	5983	185 (3.1%)		3491	255 (7.3%)		2821	498 (17.7%)
1973	5817	102 (1.8%)		3482	199 (5.7%)		2857	265 (9.3%)
4-Yr Growth	166	83		9	56		-36	+233
Women as % of total increase		33%			86%			100%

Other Institutions

	Men	Women (%)		Men	Women (%)		Men	Women (%)
1977	34115	1988 (5.8%)		27914	3013 (10.8%)		21566	4759 (22.1%)
1973	27047	1563 (5.8%)		22062	1868 (8.5%)		19075	2714 (14.2%)
4-Yr Growth	7068	425		5852	1145		2491	2045
Women as % of total increase		5.7%			16.4%			45.1%

* See Appendix B-1 for a description of ranking of institutions by R&D expenditures.

Source: Survey of Doctorate Recipients, National Research Council.
The statistics in this table are weighted estimates derived from
a sample survey of 65,000 Ph.D's in science and engineering. The
estimates are subject to two types of error - sampling and non-
sampling, (e.g., non-response bias). A discussion of the
survey is provided in Appendix D.

Tenure status is an important factor in assessing equity in academic appointments. The uneven proportions of tenured positions for men and women are shown in Table 4.16 and Figure 4.2.

We have examined the sex distribution of tenure in associate professorships in more detail. Field totals in both numbers and percents for 1975 and 1977 are shown in Table 4.17. The trends for successive Ph.D. cohorts are given in Tables 4.18A and 4.18B.

It is clear that overall, men are still somewhat more likely than women associate professors to be accorded tenure. The discrepancy increased in some fields, notably chemistry and biological sciences, from 1975 to 1977. The exceptions are the social sciences and those fields containing very few women--physics/astronomy, earth sciences, agricultural and medical sciences--for which there are also substantial fluctuations from year to year and cohort to cohort because of the small numbers of women. In the biological sciences, the overall difference remains but appears to be diminishing for the most recent cohorts. In psychology (except for the most recent cohort in 1975), mathematics and strikingly in chemistry, the male advantage with respect to tenure remains down to the latest cohort.

The fact is that despite the very recent appearance of equality in the granting of tenure to men and women in some fields, it could well be several decades before the relative proportions of men and women scientists who are tenured faculty approach equality. As the numbers in these tables indicate, women are still a minority of the new Ph.D.'s in each field and in some disciplines, a very tiny minority. Given the decline in college enrollments of the 1970's and the general tightening of opportunities for faculty advancement of both sexes, the granting of tenure to men and women faculty in equal proportion will not produce substantial changes in faculty composition for a long time to come.

Performance of Male and Female Faculty

The construction of standards for assessing the relative merits of faculty is an enterprise in which countless committees have come to grief. We will attempt not to join their ranks, but wish to note several points relevant to quality comparisons.

The desirable qualities of faculty members are usually assessed under the heading of teaching, research, and service to the institution. Women's capacity either as teachers or contributing members of the university community has not been questioned, but their research potential has.

TABLE 4.16 Tenure Status of Science and Engineering Faculty at Four-Year
Colleges and Universities by Rank and Sex, 1977

| Faculty Rank | Number and Percent in Tenured Positions | | | | |
| | Men | | | Women | |
	No.	% a		No.	% a
Professor	49,275	95.8		2,314	92.0
Associate Professor	29,784	81.6		2,638	71.4
Assistant Professor	3,458	12.6		593	10.0

a Percent is based on the number who reported tenure status.

Source: Survey of Doctorate Recipients, National Research Council. The statistics
in this table are weighted estimates, derived from a sample survey
of 65,000 Ph.D.'s in science and engineering. The estimates are
subject to two types of error -- sampling and nonsampling (e.g.,
nonresponse bias). A discussion of the survey is provided in Appendix
D.

Figure 4.2 Percent of Doctoral Science and Engineering Faculty
Holding Tenured Positions, by Rank and Sex, 1977

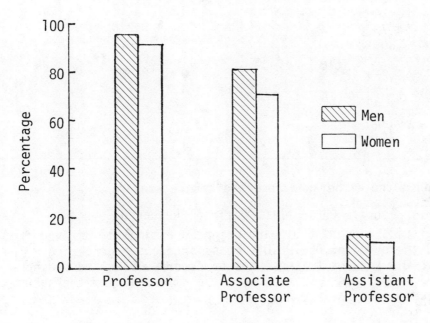

83

TABLE 4.17   Tenure Status of Associate Professors Holding Science and Engineering Ph.D's by Field of Employment and Sex in 1975 and 1977

Number and Percent *in Tenured Positions

Field of Employment	1975		1977	
	Men	Women	Men	Women
All Science and Eng. Fields	25,136 77.8	2,097 71.3	28,755 81.9	2,250 72.9
Mathematics	2,573 81.9	134 74.9	3,098 88.2	164 82.0
Computer Sciences	273 74.8	--- ---	290 68.6	15 100.0
Physics/Astron.	1,956 81.3	35 100.0	2,181 88.2	31 66.0
Chemistry	2,406 85.4	216 78.3	2,493 89.1	169 76.1
Earth Sciences	1,076 68.8	23 100.0	1,125 79.0	18 100.0
Engineering	3,054 80.4	--- ---	3,176 80.5	--- ---
Agricultural Sci.	1,555 82.7	12 100.0	1,616 81.1	12 100.0
Medical Sciences	800 63.7	133 55.0	1,162 67.6	200 65.1
Bio. Sciences	4,737 80.1	528 72.9	5,218 80.9	612 65.9
Psychology	2,274 70.8	422 65.8	2,508 77.6	485 70.6
Social Sciences	4,432 74.7	594 73.3	5,888 82.6	844 79.4

*Percent is based on the number who reported tenure status.

Source: Survey of Doctorate Recipients, National Research Council
The statistics in this table are weighted estimates, derived from
a sample survey of 65,000 Ph.D's in science and engineering. The
estimates are subject to two types of error,-- sampling and non-
sampling, (e.g., non-response bias). A discussion of the survey
is provided in Appendix D.

TABLE 4.18A   1975 Tenure Status of Associate Professors Holding Science and Engineering Doctorates by Field of Employment, Sex and Ph.D. Cohorts

Number and Percent* in Tenured Positions

Field of Employment	1950-59 Ph.Ds		1960-69 Ph.Ds		1970-72 Ph.Ds	
	Men	Women	Men	Women	Men	Women
Total	2,290	294	18,101	1,302	3,814	347
	91.7	73.1	82.6	74.0	60.3	60.0
Mathematics	149	---	1,925	103	415	19
	85.6	---	87.9	78.6	62.9	52.8
Physics/Astron.	137	12	1,655	23	164	---
	100.0	100.0	85.1	100.0	60.1	---
Chemistry	346	50	1,827	134	133	11
	100.0	100.0	84.9	75.3	61.0	40.7
Earth Sciences	85	---	831	23	160	---
	100.0	---	72.3	100.0	53.9	---
Engineering	227	---	2,444	---	317	---
	100.0	---	86.5	---	51.5	---
Agricultural Sci.	224	---	1,046	12	285	---
	100.0	---	84.9	100.0	67.1	---
Medical Sciences	115	31	510	70	156	32
	77.7	51.7	67.9	68.6	49.8	52.5
Bio. Sciences	622	95	3,416	299	526	51
	92.1	75.4	81.9	70.7	61.1	58.6
Psychology	139	66	1,737	266	398	90
	59.4	79.5	79.0	62.3	56.1	68.7
Social Sciences	246	40	2,710	372	1,260	144
	100.0	56.3	82.4	84.4	64.5	61.0

*Percent is based on the number who reported tenure status.

Note: Computer Sciences are not shown here due to the small number of cases; cohorts prior to 1950 and after 1974 have been excluded for the same reason.

Source: Survey of Doctorate Recipients, National Research Council
The statistics in this table are weighted estimates, derived from a sample survey of 65,000 Ph.D's in science and engineering. The estimates are subject to two types of error -- sampling and non-sampling, (e.g., non-response bias). A discussion of the survey is provided in Appendix D.

85

TABLE 4.18B   1977 Tenure Status of Associate Professors Holding Science and Engineering Doctorates by Field of Employment, Sex and Ph.D. Cohort

| | Number and Percent*in Tenured Positions | | | | | |
| | 1950-59 Ph.Ds | | 1960-69 Ph.Ds | | 1970-72 Ph.Ds | |
Field of Employment	Men	Women	Men	Women	Men	Women
Total	1,992	278	17,110	1,816	8,704	746
	92.4	86.1	86.6	75.8	72.6	65.4
Mathematics	139	7	1,907	111	1,002	39
	100.0	100.0	92.7	88.1	79.1	65.0
Physics/Astron.	167	7	1,568	24	391	---
	100.0	100.0	90.7	60.0	74.9	---
Chemistry	205	30	1,822	119	379	20
	100.0	100.0	90.7	76.8	76.0	54.1
Earth Sciences	38	---	731	18	356	---
	100.0	---	84.7	100.0	68.1	---
Engineering	128	---	2,229	---	779	---
	100.0	---	88.8	---	63.9	---
Agricultural Sci.	191	---	882	12	543	---
	100.0	---	83.6	100.0	72.7	---
Medical Sciences	112	38	648	71	353	57
	68.3	100.0	66.7	68.9	66.2	52.3
Bio. Sciences	625	84	3,288	352	1,182	121
	91.9	65.1	84.0	64.9	69.0	65.1
Psychology	151	45	1,438	280	919	160
	72.9	100.0	82.8	75.1	71.5	59.5
Social Sciences	236	67	2,597	389	2,800	349
	100.0	100.0	89.4	87.0	76.2	72.9

*Percent is based on the number who reported tenure status.

Note: Computer Sciences are not shown here due to the small number of cases; cohorts prior to 1950 and after 1974 have been excluded for the same reason.

Source: Survey of Doctorate Recipients, National Research Council
The statistics in this table are weighted estimates, derived from a sample survey of 65,000 Ph.D's in science and engineering. The estimates are subject to two types of error - sampling and non-sampling (e.g., non-response bias). A discussion of the survey is provided in Appendix D.

86

Estimates of research potential are based on prior productivity, ordinarily measured by publication and citation counts, the latter considered a proxy measure of quality. Citation counts suffer from a variety of well-recognized methodological problems having to do with ordering of authors' names, citations to review articles, and frequency of references to erroneous results. Productivity measures using citation counts must therefore be evaluated with caution.

Studies comparing the productivity of men and women faculty have yielded ambiguous and sometimes contradictory results. One major study of a national sample of faculty (Bayer 1970:15) found that 2 percent of the women and 11 percent of the men had published 21 or more articles, and that 63 percent of the women and 39 percent of the men had not published any research papers. These results are to be expected for a national sample, taking into account the relative distribution of male and female faculty among types of institutions and ranks documented in this chapter. Studies controlling for rank, field, and institution give quite different results, finding little or no difference in publication rates (e.g., Loeb and Ferber, Hargens) or higher publication rates for married women than for unmarried women and married or unmarried men (Simon, Clark, and Galway).

For the specific case of science faculty, factors such as access to appropriate research facilities, division of time between undergraduate and graduate teaching responsibilities, and especially availability of graduate and other research assistants may be of far greater signficance to productivity than rank or other variables which have been controlled in the studies cited above. We have not found any studies that control for these factors or indeed consider them.

As we have shown in this chapter, the distribution of women faculty in research departments is such that productivity comparisons between men and women of similar age and experience in the same field and institutions, and thus with comparable research opportunities, are virtually impossible.

A lively illustration of this difficulty is found in Career Achievements of NDEA Fellows (NRC, 1977a) which reports lower publication and citation rates for women who were National Defense Education Act fellows than for men. In nearly all fields, the average number of publications and citations for men fellows exceeded those for women by 50 percent or more. It also reports, however, a mean salary differential of approximately 25 percent for the two groups, which is far too large to be explained by sex discrimination per se. Clearly, the male and female fellows, presumably quite evenly matched at the outset, must have had different careers providing very different opportunities for research.

It appears likely that comparisons of this type serve more as indicators of inequality in initial appointments and later promotions, with attendant differences of access to graduate students, facilities, and funding, than as measures of inherent sex differences in research capability. Certainly, the most carefully controlled studies of productivity do not suggest a significant advantage for either sex.

Appointment and tenure decisions are not usually based on statistical comparisons but on individual judgments of a given person's performance. That performance may or may not be affected if the person is an isolated phenomenon, a token; none of the studies of comparative productivity have taken account of this possibility.

The dangers of tokenism cut both ways, as Kanter (1977) has pointed out: the token person may, by the pressures of being an outsider, be forced into behaving in uncharacteristic and counterproductive ways but the majority group may then respond similarly. Until an occasional major research department can assemble at least a critical mass of women faculty--something of the order of one-third of its members, according to Kanter's hypothesis--we do not believe studies of comparative performance will have much validity.

Faculty Salaries

Salary differences between men and women are widespread in all occupations and at all educational levels. Academic salaries are no exception but the extent of the differences has been difficult to determine. The reason is this: breakdowns by field, institutional category, and years of service, etc., yield so few women in most cells, at least in the sciences, that multivariate regression analyses are often required. A detailed study by Darland et al. used multivariate regression analysis with over 25 predictor variables to investigate the extent to which male/female differences could be explained by relatively objective factors, such as highest degree earned, differences in performance, etc. The study found that women were typically paid about $1500 less than the predicted salary for a man with the same attributes (Darland et al., 1973). The analyses were based on a large-scale national survey conducted by the Carnegie Commission in 1969. In this section, we will examine more recent salaries of men and women faculty, and the extent to which salary differences may have narrowed between 1973 and 1977.

In 1977 men's academic salaries overall exceeded women's by approximately 20 percent, with a slightly better record in public institutions and a slightly worse one in private ones, corresponding to other differences such as rank distribution. The magnitude of the effect is due in part to women's concentration at lower ranks, and is often ascribed to the fact that relatively more of them are in lower-paid fields. As we shall demonstrate, such deductions are not necessarily valid.

In Tables 4.19A-C we examine median salaries for men and women faculty by rank for those science fields containing enough women to make the comparison at all, and we examine as well the trends between 1973 and 1977. At the full professor level, where women have suffered larger percentage and dollar differences than in other ranks, three fields (chemistry, medical sciences, and psychology) show larger discrepancies in 1977 than in 1973. In other fields there was some reduction of the difference in 1975 followed by larger gaps in 1977. The dollar differences for men and women full professors were at least $2,500 in every field and reached $6,200 in chemistry. The trends are not the same at other ranks. We still note an increasing salary advantage for men in chemistry and fairly large differentials in the medical sciences. Two fields-- psychology and physics--show relatively small gaps at associate and assistant ranks by 1977.

When we examine the data by Carnegie Classification of institutions* as in Table 4.20, we have almost no fields left for comparison in Research Universities I and II, as might be expected from rank distributions discussed earlier. Assistant professors' salaries should show the fastest response to change, and are the ones given here for the 1970-1974 and 1975-1976 Ph.D. cohorts in 1977. Improvement for the later cohort is generally not dramatic, except in chemistry in the category of "other institutions," and in psychology in Research Universities I where there is a surprising reversal of the difference, the only one we have noted. Psychology in "other" institutions, however, has lower salaries for the more recent women doctorates, and sociology shows no significant change.

We have also examined similar data for all ranks, Ph.D. cohorts, and institutional categories. The data are not reproduced here because of their complexity, but they seem to hold no major surprises. In all cases women's salaries are lower than men's; in many areas the differentials are largest for the 1960-1969 Ph.D. cohort.

It should be pointed out here, as well, that an extraneous factor is operating to affect the salaries of

89

Table 4.19A   Trends in Median Faculty Salaries of Science Doctorates by Sex and Field, 1973-1977

Full Professors

Field of Employment*	1973			1975			1977		
	Men	Women	Diff.	Men	Women	Diff.	Men	Women	Diff.
Mathematics	$25,200 (2,677)	$22,400 (117)	12.5%	$27,500 (3,146)	$24,600 (146)	11.8%	$29,900 (3,315)	$26,800 (157)	11.6%
Chemistry	22,900 (3,186)	18,700 (126)	22.5	24,800 (4,366)	20,700 (162)	19.8	28,100 (4,394)	21,900 (201)	28.3
Medical Sciences	27,300 (1,625)	24,200 (79)	12.8	30,500 (2,207)	25,800 (140)	18.2	33,400 (2,089)	28,500 (189)	17.2
Biological Sci.	24,100 (7,169)	20,600 (533)	17.0	26,200 (7,889)	23,300 (653)	12.4	29,600 (7,797)	25,900 (510)	14.3
Psychology	24,600 (3,126)	22,900 (288)	7.4	26,800 (4,010)	25,200 (342)	6.3	30,500 (3,854)	28,000 (387)	8.9
Social Sciences	24,400 (6,720)	20,800 (354)	17.3	26,900 (8,014)	23,800 (510)	13.0	30,300 (8,289)	26,800 (553)	13.1

*Medians were not calculated for fields with fewer than 10 female respondents.

Notes: Academic salaries for 9-10 months have been adjusted to full-year equivalents. Data are for those full-time employed at four-year colleges, universities, or medical schools. Numbers in parentheses indicate weighted number of individuals reporting salary.

Source: Survey of Doctorate Recipients, National Research Council
The statistics in this table are weighted estimates, derived from a sample survey of 65,000 Ph.D.'s in science and engineering. The statistics are subject to two types of error -- sampling and non-sampling (e.g., non-response bias). A discussion of the survey is provided in Appendix D.

Table 4.19B Trends in Median Faculty Salaries of Science Doctorates by Sex and Field, 1973-1977

Associate Professors

Field of Employment*	1973			1975			1977		
	Men	Women	Diff.	Men	Women	Diff.	Men	Women	Diff.
Mathematics	$18,600 (2,424)	$17,600 (141)	5.7%	$20,300 (3,067)	$19,200 (175)	5.7%	$22,200 (3,384)	$21,500 (187)	3.3%
Physics	18,500 (1,935)	17,800 (45)	3.9	20,100 (2,449)	19,500 (44)	3.1	22,300 (2,320)	21,900 (55)	1.8
Chemistry	17,400 (2,217)	16,400 (150)	6.1	19,600 (2,715)	18,100 (240)	8.3	22,100 (2,575)	20,200 (189)	9.4
Medical Sciences	21,000 (1,036)	19,900 (137)	5.5	23,100 (1,281)	21,200 (241)	9.0	26,000 (1,599)	23,300 (276)	11.6
Biological Sci.	18,600 (5,141)	17,500 (609)	6.3	20,200 (5,724)	19,500 (648)	3.6	22,800 (5,826)	22,500 (795)	1.3
Psychology	18,500 (2,453)	18,400 (351)	0.5	20,100 (3,214)	19,800 (592)	1.5	22,300 (3,124)	22,100 (622)	0.9
Social Sciences	18,600 (4,703)	17,600 (521)	5.7	20,200 (5,812)	19,700 (769)	2.5	22,500 (6,511)	22,000 (990)	2.3

*Medians were not calculated for fields with fewer than 10 female respondents.

Note: Academic salaries for 9-10 months have been adjusted to full-year equivalents. Data are for those full-time employed at four-year colleges, universities, or medical schools. Numbers in parentheses indicate weighted number of individuals reporting salary.

Source: Survey of Doctorate Recipients, National Research Council.
The statistics in this table are weighted estimates, derived from a sample survey of 65,000 Ph.D.'s in science and engineering. The statistics are subject to two types of error -- sampling and non-sampling (e.g., non-response bias). A discussion of the survey is provided in Appendix D.

Table 4.19C Trends in Median Faculty Salaries of Science Doctorates by Sex and Field, 1973-1977

Assistant Professors

Field Employment*	1973			1975			1977		
	Men	Women	Diff.	Men	Women	Diff.	Men	Women	Diff.
Mathematics	$15,300 (2,772)	$14,600 (205)	4.8%	$16,600 (2,736)	$16,200 (207)	2.5%	$18,000 (2,322)	$17,300 (254)	4.0%
Physics	15,300 (1,631)	14,900 (66)	2.7	16,600 (1,255)	16,000 (79)	3.8	18,300 (1,368)	18,100 (71)	1.1
Chemistry	15,100 (1,732)	14,100 (140)	7.1	16,500 (1,879)	15,200 (197)	8.6	18,300 (1,931)	17,100 (255)	7.0
Medical Sciences	17,400 (1,061)	15,600 (164)	11.5	19,100 (1,259)	18,300 (261)	4.4	21,000 (1,358)	19,900 (293)	5.5
Biological Sci.	15,600 (4,803)	15,000 (756)	4.0	17,200 (5,127)	16,500 (1,154)	4.2	19,100 (5,293)	18,400 (1,361)	3.8
Psychology	15,400 (2,399)	15,300 (698)	0.6	16,600 (2,727)	16,600 (1,007)	0.0	18,100 (2,791)	18,000 (1,178)	0.6
Social Sciences	15,500 (4,169)	14,900 (637)	4.0	17,000 (5,134)	16,600 (1,058)	2.4	18,400 (5,622)	17,900 (1,469)	2.8

*Medians were not calculated for fields with fewer than 10 female respondents.

Notes: Academic salaries for 9-10 months have been adjusted to full-year equivalents. Data are for those full-time employed at four-year colleges, universities, or medical schools. Numbers in parentheses indicate weighted number of individuals reporting salary.

Source: Survey of Doctorate Recipients, National Research Council. The statistics in this table are weighted estimates, derived from a sample survey of 65,000 Ph.D.'s in science and engineering. The statistics are subject to two types of error -- sampling and non-sampling (e.g., non-response bias). A discussion of the survey is provided in Appendix D.

TABLE 4.20 Median Annual Salaries of Full-Time
Employed Assistant Professors Holding
Science Doctorates by Sex, Carnegie
Classification* of University, Field, and
Ph.D. Cohort, 1977

Research Universities I

Field+	1970-74 Ph.D.'s			1975-76 Ph.D.'s		
	Men	Women	Diff.	Men	Women	Diff.
Mathematics	$18,500 (337)	$18,400 (27)	0.5%	$17,300 (91)	---	
Biology	19,800 (711)	18,800 (127)	5.5%	17,500 (100)	---	
Psychology	18,900 (296)	18,300 (116)	3.2%	17,400 (123)	$18,000 (80)	-3.4%
Sociology	19,500 (714)	19,300 (196)	1.0%	18,300 (499)	17,000 (93)	7.1%

Research Universities II

	Men	Women	Diff.	Men	Women	Diff.
Biology	$20,000 (354)	$18,000 (44)	10.0%	$17,400 (129)	---	
Sociology	18,900 (375)	17,900 (57)	5.3%	17,600 (232)	17,500 (101)	0.6%

Other Institutions

	Men	Women	Diff.	Men	Women	Diff.
Mathematics	$18,300 (798)	$17,400 (87)	4.9%	$16,100 (493)	$15,700 (47)	2.5%
Physics	17,700 (434)	17,400 (28)	1.7%	14,500 (140)	---	
Chemistry	18,100 (780)	15,900 (104)	14.4%	17,100 (221)	17,000 (35)	0.6%
Medical Sciences	20,700 (320)	20,300 (79)	1.9%	19,000 (143)	---	
Biology	18,400 (1,773)	17,500 (394)	4.9%	16,500 (506)	16,000 (155)	3.0%
Psychology	18,200 (1,080)	18,000 (420)	1.1%	16,800 (652)	16,400 (212)	2.3%
Sociology	18,400 (1,851)	17,800 (456)	3.3%	17,600 (1,609)	17,100 (425)	2.9%

*The Carnegie classification, like the AAU and R & D rankings, rates entire institutions of higher education by indices assumed to measure quality. It distinguishes doctorate-granting institutions in terms of federal financial support and number of Ph.D.'s awarded. The two categories rated highest, Research Universities I and Research Universities II, contain 52 and 40 universities respectively (Carnegie, 1973, pp. 1-7). (Used with permission. Copyright © 1976 by the Carnegie Foundation for the Advancement of Teaching.)

+The fields shown are those in which the number of women assistant professors was sufficient to permit a breakout by classification of university.

--- Indicates fewer than 10 sample individuals reporting salary.

Note: Academic salaries for 9-10 months have been adjusted to full-year equivalents.

Source: Survey of Doctorate Recipients, National Research Council. The statistics in this table are weighted estimates, derived from a sample survey of 65,000 Ph.D's in science and engineering. The estimates are subject to two types of error - sampling and non-sampling, (e.g., non-response bias). A discussion of the survey is provided in Appendix D.

93

recent Ph.D.'s. When sex, marital status and employment sector were controlled in the NRC survey of 1971-1975 biomedical and behavioral scientists,[1] it was found that within each field, the median salaries of single men and women and married women did not differ greatly or consistently but in both fields and in every employment sector, married men (who are _most_ Ph.D.'s) earned more than the others. The differences are shown in Table 4.21. Within academic institutions, married men had a distinct salary advantage.

Discussion of Findings

In this chapter, we examined recent trends in the status of women on science faculties with respect to changes in numbers, rank, tenure, and salary, and have given some attention to changing distribution along types of institution. Complex inter-relationships among these factors make it difficult to define and evaluate real change. Equality in employment, promotion, and salary presupposes that individuals are comparable in ability, and in most universities and many colleges, ability is defined largely in terms of research productivity. The latter is critically dependent, in the case of experimental sciences, on the particular institutional environment. Studies comparing research productivity of men and women show little or no difference when properly controlled for field and institutional category (in addition to the more obvious variables of age, rank, etc.). but none have taken account of uniquely important factors such as accessibility of research funding, graduate students, or research assistants. The majority of women scientists are not in the institutions where most research is done, and not in positions with opportunities for independent research initiatives.

Nonetheless, it is clear that the increase in women Ph.D.'s which began in the sixties has been followed by an increase in their presence among science faculties. The gains in total numbers of new academic positions for women scientists, and especially the gains in tenured positions, are modest, and indeed almost invisible when viewed as a fraction of the total of approximately 120,000 faculty positions. But in the top research universities, with a steady or declining population, there have been some quite real increases, and that fact has importance beyond the magnitude of the numbers. These are the institutions which are the pace-setters, and the finding that women account for 35 percent of the growth in their science faculties since 1973 is important. In view of the very limited numbers of available positions in most of these departments, and of their very high quality standards, the large fraction of women in these new positions is evidence of a different climate of opportunity. Perhaps the most important aspect

TABLE 4.21   Median Salaries of 1971-1975 Ph.D.'s Who Are Employed Full-Time or Hold Postdoctoral Appointments by Sex, Marital Status, and Employment Sector

	Post-doctorals	Full-Time Employed Total	Acad.	Govt.	Indust.	Other Sector
Biomedical Sciences Ph.D.'s						
Men						
Married	$12,200	$20,200	$19,600	$22,100	$23,300	$20,600
Single	12,000	18,500	17,800	20,200	22,900	19,600
Marital Status Unknown	14,200	20,000	19,200	*	*	*
Women						
Married	11,900	18,100	17,600	20,200	21,400	*
Single	11,500	18,200	17,900	21,400	*	*
Marital Status Unknown	*	*	*	*	*	*
Behavioral Sciences Ph.D.'s						
Men						
Married	13,200	20,100	19,600	21,600	25,300	20,800
Single	11,200	19,600	18,400	19,900	21,000	19,600
Marital Status Unknown	*	20,600	20,000	*	*	*
Women						
Married	11,500	18,600	18,200	19,200	19,900	20,000
Single	11,200	18,300	17,900	20,500	*	18,500
Marital Status Unknown	*	*	*	*	*	*

*Median salaries based on fewer than 20 survey responses are not reported.

SOURCE: Survey of Biomedical and Behavioral Scientists, National Research Council

to note is that we are witnessing the gradual reversal of a very old tradition in these institutions.

These changes have not occurred uniformly in all fields. In earth sciences, where total numbers of women are still very small, they have increased dramatically; in engineering, with still smaller numbers, the increase is almost as large but does not attain statistical significance. The smallest changes, which are however also statistically insignificant, have occurred in chemistry and mathematics. In the latter two fields the proportions of women faculty at leading institutions are strikingly at variance with the relatively large doctoral pool. A very few, very recent appointments in leading chemistry departments (Rawls and Fox, 1978) may, however, be the beginning of a new trend.

It has been suggested that the apparent persistent sex biases in chemistry and mathematics departments may result from different distributions of the sexes among subfields. For example, if women chemists disproportionately prefer the "softer" parts of their discipline or women mathematicians the less rigorous fields of theirs, then they may not in fact be eligible for the job openings which arise. The available facts do not support this interpretation. An examination of the distribution of men and women doctorates among the subfields of the two disciplines in recent years (Harmon, 1977, Appendix A) shows them to be essentially identical except that in chemistry, women tend to slightly favor the specialties traditionally regarded as more rigorous, and to be significantly less likely than men to specialize in organic chemistry (about one-fourth of the women and one-third of the men specialized in this in 1974). A future study would do well to examine in detail the situations in mathematics and chemistry which seem to have special problems.

In the great majority of colleges and universities that are not among the leading research institutions, the numbers of women have increased at comparable rates. Here, as in the top institutions, the proportion of women assistant professors has nearly doubled. Their rate of promotion to associate professorships corresponds roughly to the average proportion of women among assistant professors over the four-year period, while in the research universities that rate is very much higher.

The lag in the granting of tenure to women, however, has persisted throughout the period under examination. It becomes most evident in the "other" category of institutions where the fraction of women promoted to full professorships in all the sciences is actually slightly below their already low presence in that group. A slower advancement of women at the "other" institutions may be, in part, due to a transfer of the best women at these institutions to the more prestigious ones.

Differences in the salaries of men and women faculty have followed the general trend toward equalization, though change in this factor is bound to be less rapid when women constitute large fractions of the new entrants to each rank. A notable exception occurs in chemistry, where the salary differential has increased for all ranks, and in medical sciences for full and associate professors. As already noted in Chapter 3, salary discrimination is especially serious because it is usually covert and cumulative.

It is also hard to justify even on economic grounds: given the small numbers of women in most fields, the actual cost of correcting blatant inequalities would be small. Among full professors of chemistry, where the difference in median salaries of men and women is far greater than in any other category, the added salary costs (excluding benefits) for men between 1973 and 1977 were about $50 million; the difference between the actual salaries paid to women professors in 1977 and the potential cost if their median salaries had been equal to men's would have been about $1.2 million. Spread over four years and dozens of institutions, that cost is not prohibitive.

More detailed studies of salary equity are beyond the constraints of this report. The data of the Survey of Doctorate Recipients, however, could well be the subject of a more extended analysis offering the possibility of relating salaries to length of service. Such a study is likely to shed some light on the flow-through or "revolving door" assistant professorship; if disproportionately high fractions of women assistant professors (compared to their hiring and promotion rates) are found to have entry level salaries, that would be an indication of abnormally high turnover.

What of affirmative action policies? There is no doubt, in our judgment, that the existence of equal opportunity laws, regardless of their actual enforcement, is primarily responsible for the relative increase in the numbers of women faculty and also for the relative improvement in salaries, at least at the entry level. Current efforts to simplify and strengthen affirmative action enforcement have our full support. Particular attention needs to be paid to both tenure and salary equalization; internal initiatives with departments and institutions are preferable by far to legal action. The costs of the latter for institutions are likely to be higher than the cost of the necessary salary adjustments themselves. For aggrieved individuals, the price of legal action is often measured in irreparable damage to professional prospects as well as in dollars they cannot afford.

NOTES

1 Private communications to Committee members. Among institutions that have expressed concern over this problem are Yale, Cornell, Indiana University, Princeton, the University of Minnesota, the University of California-all campuses, Stanford, and Purdue.

2 Private communication, Higher Education Resource Services.

3 This is not directly comparable to the ranking of institutions by R&D expenditures which we have used elsewhere, but serves as a reasonable approximation for this purpose. See the explanation of the classification in Appendix B-2.

4 The salary tabulation was specially prepared for this report.

CHAPTER 5

PARTICIPATION IN THE NATIONAL SCIENCE
ADVISORY APPARATUS

The Federal government has been seeking formal advice
from scientists on issues concerning national policy since
the establishment of the National Academy of Sciences for
that purpose during the Civil War. During World War II, and
especially during the Sputnik era, advisory bodies dealing
with science-related issues proliferated. By the nature of
their origins and purposes, they were concerned largely with
military and national-security questions, and therefore
consisted predominantly of physical scientists and
engineers. Advisory groups dealing with problems in the
life and social science areas evolved quite recently, by
comparison. Peer review groups, which evaluate fellowship
and research grant applications, have had a similar history.

Membership of policy advisory bodies is drawn primarily
from the ranks of senior faculty and senior research and
technical management personnel in industry. Peer review
groups, on the other hand, also contain younger and less
well established scientists who are themselves active in the
research areas concerned.

Both peer review and policy advisory groups can have
considerable influence on the course of science, though
naturally in different ways. Although peer reviews of
research grants and fellowship applications are made on
scientific merit alone, different individuals may view merit
from different perspectives, and the sum of reviewers'
ratings results in quality judgments that will help to
determine which applications are funded and therefore, how
policy is in fact carried out. Policy advisory groups, by
definition, act in a much broader sphere, and their findings
and recommendations set the stage for policy-making bodies
such as the National Science Board or the Office of Science
and Technology Policy. Certain kinds of advisory committees
deserve special mention. These are groups whose primary
task is problem-solving, formulation of a scientific
judgment drawn from existing data which have not been
previously synthesized in a way that makes possible the
definition of public policy. Examples of this sort of task
are recommendations dealing with fluorocarbons in the upper

99

atmosphere, regulation of recombinant DNA research, or the setting of radiation exposure standards. Members of all such advisory bodies therefore have opportunities to delineate policies which affect the development of individual science fields, the priorities among them, and the allocation of public funds to various research areas. Beyond the immediate effects on science, such policies then may have broad impact on society--on jobs, environment and quality of life. Participation in advisory bodies also provides more personal benefits for the members; they become better known and more visible, gain early knowledge of impending research developments or policy changes, and can put that knowledge to use in their own work. It has been pointed out that participation in advisory panels may also help to raise the status of members at their home institutions (Apter, 1973, p. 104).

In the hierarchy of science policy advisory groups, peer review committees, site-visit teams, and a variety of specialized subcommittees are the farm teams for the major leagues (the many boards and commissions that deal with more explicit science policy issues on a broader scale). Here is where younger scientists are trained to become policymakers and where they learn not only how to be effective in a new environment but also how to find their way to and through the funding agencies. This process also allows committee chairpersons and other experienced participants to survey the new entrants and judge their capabilities for further service.

The extent to which women have had, or now have, opportunities to participate in the shaping of national science policy is not easy to determine with accuracy. Members of advisory bodies have not been studied as regularly as have new doctorates or the professoriate. Although one major study (NRC, 1972) has reviewed the history of science advising, analyzed the varieties of committees which contribute to this field, and made a number of recommendations including greater emphasis on recruiting younger scientists, women, and minority group members for science committee service, no comprehensive definition of science advisory groups exists, and there are no extensive data on their composition. Nonetheless, we believe it is important to assess whether women have opportunities both to be heard in the science policy arena and to derive the usual rewards in prestige and experience from such service. We are therefore including this section with the caveat that the information available is limited and should be viewed as a first approximation. Little in the way of historical comparisons is possible; data on the sex composition of advisory groups are available only for the immediate past and only for some kinds of groups. This overview, then, may serve as a starting point for future assessments.

100

A more detailed taxonomy of science committees than is necessary to our purposes is given in the NAS report cited above. It distinguishes a "technical committee" which requires only appropriate technical expertise from its members and is thus particularly suitable as an instrument for the introduction of new recruits to committee service (NRC, 1972, p. 14).

In 1970 a total of 57 women served on NRC committees, constituting about one percent of all committee members (NRC, 1972, Appendix D, p. 47). The figure for the National Science Foundation was 7 or 1.9 percent and in 1972, 28 women or 1.4 percent, served on committees of the National Institutes of Health (Apter, 1973, p. 104).

Data Sources

Peer review panels are generally assembled by the officers of the programs under review, and are drawn from the whole spectrum of disciplines in which grant programs operate. Their composition is thus determined within the relevant agencies. Policy-level bodies may come into existence in various ways, but a common mechanism is to request the National Academy of Sciences, through the National Research Council, to appoint an appropriate group. Some advisory groups, however, are appointed directly by the agencies requesting their services.

Because of the difficulties of obtaining comparable data from many and diverse sources, we have not attempted a comprehensive review of all national science advisory bodies, but have focused on four major groups closely related to academic science--the National Academy of Sciences-National Research Council, the National Institutes of Health, the Alcohol, Drug Abuse, and Mental Health Administration (ADAMHA), and the National Science Foundation. Data are derived from published membership lists and were furnished directly to the Committee by officers of the NRC and the agencies. Record keeping varies with the institution and at present is probably most sophisticated at the National Institutes of Health where information is computerized and the coding system permits detailed analysis of membership patterns. A portion of the National Science Foundation data is also computerized. ADAMHA, with smaller numbers of committee members, and NAS rely on manual tabulations.

National Academy of Sciences - National Research Council

The National Academy of Sciences and its sister organizations, the National Academy of Engineering and the Institute of Medicine, are honorary associations whose members elect their colleagues by a rather complex process. As such, they are outside the scope of this review. The public advisory functions of the Academies are performed largely (but not exclusively) through the National Research Council (NRC), and Academy members play an important role in these functions. In addition, public reports of NRC committees are subject to review by the Academy's Report Review Committee. Academy members are, therefore, influential in science policy decisions at many levels by virtue of their membership status as well as their scientific eminence. For that reason, an assessment of recent changes in membership patterns of women is relevant to our purpose. Women as a percentage of members of the three organizations are shown in Table 5.1. The numbers of women members of the recently established Institute of Medicine (1970) and the National Academy of Engineering (1964) reflect with reasonable accuracy the representation of women in these professions at levels which would make them eligible for membership. The situation is rather different in the National Academy of Sciences (founded 1863), which elected its first woman member in 1925 and a total of ten women in its first 107 years, prior to 1970. Since then the increase in women members has been explosive by comparison, reaching a total of 33 living members in 1978, or 2.6 percent of all members. In 1977, four new women members were elected, representing 6.7 percent of all new members and in 1978, women were 8.3 percent of the new members.

For readers not familiar with the lengthy nomination and election procedures of NAS it should be pointed out that the process may take several years. The fact that the rate of election of women members began to rise rapidly in 1970 therefore indicates that the scientific community had set in motion the process of according more women scientists this recognition well before any explicit requirements for affirmative action arose. It should also be noted that this happened long before the growing numbers of new women doctorates could possibly be of sufficient age to be included in any reasonable pool of potential Academy members. Stated differently, this means that the women scientists now being elected to membership come from the accumulated pool of earlier years, when women represented a much smaller fraction of all scientists. The percentage of new women members now closely parallels that of women on senior faculties.

Women scientists are unevenly distributed in the leadership of the academies, as shown in Table 5.2. With most women members having only been elected recently, this is not altogether surprising. If we exclude IOM, however, women are only minimally represented in leadership positions. While we do not believe it useful to argue a need for proportional representation at this level, we do

TABLE 5.1   The Participation of Women in the
                            Membership of the National Academies

                                    1977 - 1978

	Total	Women	% Women
National Academy of Sciences (NAS)	1,215	33	2.6
National Academy of Engineering (NAE)	765	7	0.9
Institute of Medicine (IOM)	298	33	11.1

Source: Organization and Members, 1977-1978, National Academy of Sciences,
         National Academy of Engineering, Institute of Medicine, National
         Research Council, National Academy of Sciences, Washington, October
         1977.

express the hope that as more women members are elected,
their presence among the leadership will also increase.

   Academy membership is not a requirement for service on
the four assemblies and four commissions of the National
Research Council, or on the numerous boards, panels, and
committees which report to them. In fact, of the total 2616
NRC appointments for terms beginning in 1977, only 420 or 16
percent were of NAS, NAE, or IOM members. We would
therefore expect participation by women in these activities
to be higher than their membership ratio, reflecting their
much greater presence among research scientists, especially
in the social sciences which are relevant to much ongoing
work of the assemblies and commissions. By and large this
expectation is fulfilled, as Tables 5.3 and 5.4 show.

   Women accounted for 178 of the total 2616 appointments
in 1977-1978, or 5.3 percent. This is somewhat higher than
their overall NRC participation for this and the preceding
year (see Table 5.5) and represents a rising rate of
appointments. Normally, appointments are made for three-
year terms so that on the average only one-third turn over
annually. The rate at which women are now being appointed
is therefore close to their rate of election to NAS
membership.

TABLE 5.2　　　　　　　　　The Participation of Women in the
　　　　　　　　　　　　　Leadership of the National Academies

1977 - 1978

	Total	Women	% Women
Councillors of the National Academy of Sciences	17	1	6
Councillors of the National Academy of Engineering	17	0	0
Councillors of the Institute of Medicine	22	2	9.1
National Research Council Governing Board	14	0	0
Chairpersons of Major Divisions	14	0	0
Total	84	3	3%

If the Institute of Medicine is excluded, the percentage of women in the leadership is 1%.

Source: Organization and Members, 1977-1978, National Academy of Sciences, National Academy of Engineering, Institute of Medicine, National Research Council, National Academy of Sciences, Washington, October 1977.

It should be remembered, however, that the criteria for committee membership differ from those for election to the Academy. Committee activity involves the broader participation of social scientists and psychologists of whom 14 percent and 23 percent, respectively, are now women (Table 2.8). It is also instructive to examine the current appointment figure of 5.3 percent in relation to the representation of women in the appropriate pool which, for this purpose, we may define as the 1955-1965 doctoral cohort. Women received 7.3 percent of the science and engineering Ph.D.'s during that period (Gilford and Snyder, 1977, p. 24). The percentage of current appointments is still below that figure.

The complete absence of women from the Commissions on Natural Resources and on Sociotechnical Systems is especially surprising. Not only are there many eminent women scientists in fields relevant to these Commissions,

TABLE 5.3 Participation in National Research Council Committees, 1977-1978

	Number of Committees Subcommittees and Panels	Number of Participants	Number of Women	Percent of Women
Assembly of Behavioral and Social Sciences	20	220	24	12.0%
Assembly of Engineering	48	511	14	2.7
Assembly of Life Sciences	77	684	56	8.2
Assembly of Mathematical and Physical Sciences	138	1,161	44	3.8
Commission on Human Resources[1]	39	320	43	13.4
Commission on International Relations	21	206	15	7.3
Commission on Natural Resources	37	380	16	4.2
Commission on Sociotechnical Systems	79	905	22	2.4
Total	459	4,387	234	5.3%

[1]The figures for the Commission on Human Resources do not include the Committee on the Education and Employment of Women in Science and Engineering which has 9 women members out of 13.

Source: Organization and Members, 1977-1978, National Academy of Sciences, National Academy of Engineering, Institute of Medicine, National Research Council, National Academy of Sciences, Washington, D.C., October 1977.

105

TABLE 5.4   Participation in Executive Committees
              of Assemblies and Commissions

	Number of Participants	Number of Women	Percent of Women
Assembly of Behavioral and Social Sciences	18	4	22.2%
Assembly of Engineering	20	1	5.0
Assembly of Life Sciences	15	1	6.7
Assembly of Mathematical and Physical Sciences	19	1	5.3
Commission on Human Resources	15	2	13.3
Commission on International Relations	10	2	20.0
Commission on Natural Resources	14	0	0
Commission on Sociotechnical Systems	11	0	0
Total	122	11	9.1%

Source: <u>Organization and Members, 1977-1978, National Academy of Sciences, National Academy of Engineering, Institute of Medicine, National Research Council</u>, National Academy of Sciences, Washington, D.C., October 1977.

TABLE 5.5   The Participation of Women on National Research Council
             Bodies, 1975-1978*

	1975	1976	1977	1978
Total Individuals	7,888	7,658	7,484	7,638
Women	311	303	347	391
Percent	3.9%	4.0%	4.6%	5.1%

*The figures show participation as of approximately June 30 during each of the years and are believed to be reasonably comparable. They summarize the numbers of individuals serving, rather than appointments which involve some duplication. All levels of NRC bodies are included since the Office of the President of NAS does not tabulate membership by sex for different structural levels within NRC. Thus, the figure for 1978, 5.1 percent, reflects participation at all levels and is slightly lower than the 5.3 percent shown in Table 5.3 for committee participation, which was obtained by tabulating the information in the NAS directory, Organization and Members.

Source: Memorandum from S. D. Cornell to P. Handler, October 1978.

but the topics of interest have such broad public impact that it seems unlikely that women scientists experienced in these areas cannot be found.

Without going into excessive numerical detail, it is evident that the membership lists of the NRC Board and panels charged with studying environmental problems--"society's conflicting demands on environmental values" (NAS, 1977, p. 128)--include almost no women, in an area which is replete with women scientists and in which women have been especially active as concerned and informed citizens.

National Science Foundation

The National Science Foundation's several Directorates each have an advisory committee and these in turn have subcommittees. In addition, some directorates primarily utilize peer reviewers for handling proposals. NSF is covered by the Federal Advisory Committee Act of 1972 which requires "the membership of the advisory committee to be fairly balanced in terms of the points of view represented and the functions to be performed by the advisory committee" (Sec. 5.b.2). This provision may be interpreted in various ways within the several directorates in their selection of committee members. Nonetheless, as Table 5.6 shows, there has been a steady increase in the numbers and proportions of women committee members over the last few years, to a level that exceeds their representation in the scientific doctorate pool. It has been suggested that Congressional oversight and Foundation leadership have played a crucial part in this change.[1]

Table 5.7 shows the sex distribution of peer reviewers for the last two years, the period during which the data have been computerized. A comparison of the two years shows an overall increase in the proportion of reviews solicited from women. This also occurred in every directorate except AAEO and MPE. Interestingly, in 1978 in every directorate except Science Education, women completed a higher proportion of reviews than the proportion of reviews solicited from them.

TABLE 5.6   Sex Composition of National Science Foundation Advisory Committees 1972-1977

YEAR	NUMBER OF MEMBERS	NUMBER OF WOMEN	PERCENT WOMEN
FY 1972	358	14	4
FY 1973	389	33	8
FY 1974	411	32	8
CY 1975	652	67	10
CY 1976	747	81	11
CY 1977	926	131	14

Data furnished by Becky Winkler, Committee Management Coordinator, National Science Foundation

TABLE 5.7 Analysis of Peer Reviewers for the National Science Foundation by Directorate and Reviewer Sex, FY 1977 and FY 1978[+]

Solicited Reviews[++]

	NSF #Revs.	NSF %Total	AAEO #Revs.	AAEO %Total	MPE #Revs.	MPE %Total	BBS #Revs.	BBS %Total	ASRA #Revs.	ASRA %Total	SE #Revs.	SE %Total	STIA #Revs.	STIA %Total
Total Male FY 77	116,612	92.5	14,352	96.1	28,592	98.1	47,275	92.0	4,933	95.0	18,842	83.2	2,608	93.0
Total Male FY 78*	143,382	89.7	16,960	96.5	29,712	98.4	60,704	88.0	3,498	93.6	29,025	81.5	3,477	92.5
Change + −	+26,770	+23.0	+ 2,608	+18.2	+ 1,120	+ 3.9	+13,429	+ 28.4	- 1,435	−19.1	+10,183	+54.0	+ 869	+33.3
Total Female FY 77	9,474	7.5	586	3.9	543	1.9	4,089	8.0	257	5.0	3,804	16.8	195	7.0
Total Female FY 78*	16,438	10.3	624	3.5	469	1.6	8,254	12.0	238	6.4	6,570	18.5	283	7.5
Change + −	+ 6,964	+73.5	+ 38	+ 6.5	− 74	-13.6	+ 4,165	+101.9	− 19	- 7.4	+ 2,766	+72.7	+ 88	+45.1

Completed Reviews

	NSF #Revs.	NSF %Total	AAEO #Revs.	AAEO %Total	MPE #Revs.	MPE %Total	BBS #Revs.	BBS %Total	ASRA #Revs.	ASRA %Total	SE #Revs.	SE %Total	STIA #Revs.	STIA %Total
Total Male FY 77	92,232	92.3	12,732	92.4	24,214	98.1	30,282	92.4	4,131	95.1	18,466	83.1	2,400	93.0
Total Male FY 78*	120,149	89.3	14,847	87.6	24,772	98.4	45,570	87.6	2,825	93.3	28,937	81.6	3,192	92.2
Change + −	+27,917	+30.3	+ 2,115	+16.6	+ 558	+ 2.3	+15,288	+ 50.5	- 1,306	−31.6	+10,471	+56.7	+ 792	+33.0
Total Female FY 77	7,656	7.7	548	7.6	460	1.9	2,498	7.6	212	4.9	3,757	16.9	181	7.0
Total Female FY 78*	14,452	10.7	572	12.4	392	1.6	6,479	12.4	202	6.7	6,537	18.4	270	7.8
Change + −	+ 6,796	+88.8	+ 24	+ 4.4	− 68	-14.8	+ 3,981	+159.4	− 10	- 4.7	+ 2,780	+74.0	+ 89	+49.2

[+]Data furnished by Joan Humphries, Deputy Director, Office of Equal Employment Opportunity, National Science Foundation

*10/1/77 through 8/31/78

[++]The data actually refer to individual reviewers, rather than total reviews. Some efforts are made to restrict excessive use of individuals.

NSF = Total for the Foundation (including "other" Directorates which are not shown here).

AAEO = Astronomical, Atmospheric, Earth and Ocean Sciences

MPE = Mathematics, Physics and Engineering

BBS = Biological, Behavioral and Social Sciences

ASRA = Applied Science and Research Applications

SE = Science Education

STIA = Scientific, Technological and International Affairs

National Institutes of Health

A special tabulation of the sex composition of the membership of the 91 NIH public advisory committees in September 1978 showed women to hold 19.3 percent of the appointments (Table 5.8). The figure appears to be a most respectable one in comparison with the figures for NSF and NRC. It is higher than the current percent in the labor force of women holders of doctorates in the biological sciences, 16 percent, and higher than the 13 percent of those with degrees in the medical sciences (Table 2.8) especially when it is recalled that a large proportion of these women hold relatively recent degrees. At the same time, several considerations need to be borne in mind. The life sciences, with appropriately greater represesentation at NIH than at NAS or NSF, have a substantially higher representation of women than other sciences, except psychology and the social sciences. Secondly, the tabulation includes some lay persons, who are appointed as public representatives to some committees and some specialists in non-scientific fields, such as education and hospital administration. Finally, it should be pointed out that there are numerous committee members with professional degrees and some participation by those without advanced degrees. The ADAMHA distribution reveals even higher participation by women on committees, with a figure of 29 percent for late 1978 (Table 5.8). The proportion is substantially higher than the 14 percent of women social scientists in the labor force (Table 2.8). In addition to social scientists, and especially psychologists, however, ADAMHA committee membership includes substantial representation of psychiatrists, social workers and staff members of drug abuse, alcohol or mental health centers and clinics.

Inspection of the various levels and types of NIH and ADAMHA committees reveals variation in the participation of women according to committee function and composition (U.S. Public Health Service, 1978a and 1978b). There is greater representation of women at the higher levels of the NIH and ADAMHA structure on committees that are required to include representatives of the public or of an affected population (e.g., the population affected by sickle cell anemia). Thus, the policy-level advisory committees show higher proportions of women participants than the initial review bodies or the boards of scientific counselors who review intramural research programs within each institute.

The current representation of women on NIH committees has been attributed to two factors: costly litigation (Association for Women in Science, et al. vs. Elliot Richardson, et al.) and the centralized structure of the Institutes that permits close monitoring of appointment procedures to assure the inclusion of women and minorities.

110

TABLE 5.8 Number and Percent of Women Participating in Advisory Committees, 1975-1978

Quarter Ending September 30	Policy and Program Advisory Councils, Boards, Committees		Program and Project Advisory Committees		Initial Grant Review		Contract Review		Initial Grant and Contract Review		Boards of Scientific Counselors		Total	
	No.	%	No.	%	No.	%	No.	%	No.	%	No.	%	No.	%
National Institutes of Health (NIH)*														
1975	(54)	29.8	(24)	18.6	(207)	19.9	(66)	17.8	(25)	23.6	(15)	25.0	(391)	20.7
1976	(54)	29.5	(23)	16.7	(185)	17.5	(59)	16.8	(51)	21.8	(11)	16.9	(383)	18.9
1977	(60)	25.9	(17)	15.3	(175)	15.9	(49)	17.9	(46)	21.2	(17)	22.7	(354)	18.1
1978	(61)	25.0	(19)	19.2	(163)	15.7	(41)	19.6	(72)	24.7	(21)	27.6	(377)	19.3
Alcohol, Drug Abuse, and Mental Health Administration (ADAMHA)+														
1975	(9)	50.0	(3)	30.0	(83)	31.3++	**	**	**	**	(2)	33.3	(97)	33.4
1976	(12)	30.7	(8)	57.1	(117)	31.4	**	**	**	**	(2)	33.3	(139)	32.3
1977	(12)	27.2	(10)	62.5	(128)	29.5	**	**	**	**	(1)	20.0	(151)	30.3
1978	(9)	23.6	(10)	55.5	(97)	28.1	**	**	**	**	(2)	28.5	(118)	29.0

*Data furnished by Suzanne L. Fremeau, Committee Management Officer, NIH.

+Data furnished by Elizabeth A. Connolly, Committee Management Officer, and Donna Ricucci, Committee Management Assistant, ADAMHA.

**Contract review is not handled through advisory committees at ADAMHA.

++The percentages for women on ADAMHA advisory committees are inflated by the members of the Rape Prevention and Control Advisory Committee which now has six women members out of eight.

This procedure is regularly allowed at NIH and ADAMHA with a concerted effort to interpret the "balance" of the Federal Advisory Act to apply to women and minorities. An additional appointment stricture, designed to prevent excessive utilization of a limited number of scientists, is the rule that a committee member have a minimum break in service of at least one year before appointment to another committee. It is recognized at NIH, however, that this rule is more frequently waived for women and minority appointees.[2]

As part of its procedure for monitoring appointments, the Committee Management Office of NIH has computerized data that would permit the kinds of detailed analyses of the participation of women scientists that are beyond the scope of the present report but might be usefully undertaken in the future. (Some of these studies have been conducted at NIH, and trend data are maintained.) As currently coded, for example, these data would permit analysis by sex of the percentages of appointees who have accepted or declined appointment, distribution according to types of degrees, the proportion of appointees who have held prior appointments to NIH committees, the employment sector of appointees, and committee members' rank in their employing institutions.

An Overburden on Women Scientists?

In view of the rather recent emphasis on having women scientists represented on advisory bodies, a concern has been raised in some quarters that women scientists may be overburdened by requests for service which are hard to deny. The obvious potential problem is that with a rather small pool of women with appropriate backgrounds, a few scientists will be called on excessively with possible detriment to their research and other obligations. Certainly, for historical reasons, the list of qualified females could not have been very long. Some women may have had to turn down invitations and may have elected to give first priority to their own research rather than to advisory service.

This concern may well be justified. NRC records for 1975 show that women held 367 of a total of 8462 advisory appointments, but that unduplicated totals for this period were 311 out of 7888. Over 15 percent of women's appointments, but only 6.4 percent of men's, therefore represented duplicate or multiple service.

These figures do reflect a disproportionate burden on a few women scientists, although we have data only for one year and do not know how widespread or persistent this problem is. A cursory examination of the lists of women members of NIH advisory committees also showed some duplication of NRC committee participatants. A study of multiple committee service by women would therefore require a cross-comparison of the rosters of various national scientific bodies.

Discussion

Three issues are of concern regarding the participation of women scientists on science policy advisory bodies, the most obvious of which is equality of professional opportunity and recognition for women scientists. Secondly, we must make some educated guesses regarding the size of the pool of potential women committee members, particularly for technical committees where the dominant qualification sought is expertise in a sometimes narrow field. Less clear is the question of whether advisory bodies dominated by men may arrive at conclusions which differ from those potentially reached by sex-balanced bodies, and whether such a potential flaw adversely affects the usefulness of their decisions.

Equality of Professional Opportunities

The participation rate of women scientists in top-level advisory groups is roughly comparable to their representation among senior faculties, but we have already seen that the latter group is very small for historical reasons. No very precise comparisons are possible in any case since participation varies so widely by fields and with individual advisory bodies. The enhancement of professional opportunities for women at this level is probably not a major consideration, although public recognition and the opportunity to serve the nation are important even to those who have already achieved eminence in their fields. For this reason we believe that more women scientists should be serving in high-level advisory groups. The appropriate pool is certainly large enough to furnish additional candidates at this time, and is growing rapidly.

Women scientists qualified to serve on a variety of policy groups may have to be sought in non-traditional ways and places. For example, women who have served with distinction in small colleges or in research institutes may find themselves outside the usual recruitment channels, though fully suited by experience, maturity, and interest to take part in advisory activities. We recognize, of course, that recruitment of potential committee members is a delicate task and has entirely legitimate concerns with personal compatibility and ease of collaboration in addition to high scientific competence. Convenors of committees, therefore, tend to place great reliance on personal acquaintance for recommendations; most suitable women scientists are not really outside this network. They simply

have been overlooked more often than men in the past, and
should now be sought out more purposefully.

The low participation rate in lower-level advisory
functions and the overburdening of a few women scientists
are probably closely linked. If women are untried in these
positions, those who have already been tested are probably
seen as more desirable or predictable candidates. As we
have shown in earlier chapters, however, there is a much
larger pool of appropriately situated women scientists than
NRC is utilizing in this way. Inadequate use of women
scientists at these levels now will insure their continued
paucity at top levels since it denies them the opportunities
to learn how the game is played. It also deprives them of
experience, recognition, and rewards which would in
themselves further their careers. With frequent turnover of
membership at this level and with the frequent appointment
of ad hoc and short-term advisory groups, increasing the
utilization of women scientists would be a simple matter.
We strongly urge that this be done.

Highly specialized technical committees may occasionally
encounter problems in locating women members, depending on
the specialty involved. It is quite clear that in certain
subfields of the physical sciences, and quite probably in
other specialized areas as well, women with the requisite
expert background may literally not exist.

Sex-balanced Committees?

There are no data which suggest that women scientists as
a group draw conclusions and make decisions any differently
than men scientists. However, it is not only possible but
likely that on many science-related issues they may base
conclusions on different or additional kinds of evidence,
and if that is so then final decisions may indeed be
different if women play a part in them. For example, among
major social issues which are addressed by science advisory
groups, those dealing with health, nutrition, and family
planning (either nationally or world-wide) or with
environmental problems are very likely to be viewed from
different perspectives by men and women because of large
differences in their respective experiences in society.
Whether such differences would lead committees to make
better judgments is not something that can be predicted;
perhaps they would simply consider a wider range of options.

In an era when science policy decisions are increasingly
under public scrutiny and must be more responsive to public
perceptions of their impact than in the past, it seems
insensitive, at the least, to ignore half the public.
Decisions about energy policy, conservation, recombinant DNA
research, health, or chemicals in the environment affect

114

women as much as men. Women are especially active in consumer groups concerned with such problems. Women scientists work in these areas as often as in others. It is at least possible that their fuller participation in the policy advisory mechanism would lead to policy recommendations which are both sound and more acceptable to the public.

Conclusions and Recommendations

We are encouraged to note that the rate of election of women to the National Academy of Sciences, the National Academy of Engineering, and the Institute of Medicine during the last few years is beginning to approach the current presence of women scientists at levels commensurate with such recognition. We trust that the rate of increase will keep pace with the growing numbers of women scientists who achieve distinction, and that their greater representation will also shortly afford them more opportunities for leadership within the Academies and the National Research Council. We are encouraged by recent changes in the representation of women on committees of NIH, ADAMHA, and NSF and to a lesser extent, among the NSF peer reviewers.

At the lower levels of science policy advisory service, we are concerned at the underutilization of women scientists in general and the overburdening of a few. Given the broad range of fields involved, there are literally many hundreds of women scientists fully fitted by experience and achievement to serve on these bodies. Further, the turnover rate for such service is high enough to permit much more rapid growth in women's participation than has been realized so far. We urge an increase in the rate of appointment of women scientists to such positions with expansion to keep pace with their increasing representation in the doctorate pool.

While we commend the establishment of a "Talent Bank" or resource file for new appointments which the Commission on Human Resources is currently considering, we urge that recruitment efforts for women go well beyond such a file. Specific nominations solicited for specific purposes are, in our judgment, likely to produce more viable candidates and serve the additional objective of keeping the scientific community aware of the need to augment women scientists' careers in this fashion.

We would also suggest that a new form of record keeping would assist the NRC in identifying the areas in which progress has been uneven so that greater efforts may be exerted there.

NOTES

1   by Herbert Harrington, Director, Office of Equal
     Employment Opportunity, National Science Foundation.

2   This paragraph is based on statements made by Suzanne L.
     Fremeau, Committee Management Officer, NIH.

CHAPTER 6

PERSPECTIVES & PROSPECTS

This study indicates that the status of women Ph.D.'s in academic science has improved in the past decade, but that further gains are necessary before equal opportunity is realized.

The assessments of equal opportunity in this report have centered on the recent doctorate population, essentially those scientists who completed their education in 1970 and later. The date is merely a convenient marker in a long transition from growing awareness of possible sex discrimination through the passage of equal opportunity laws, the appearance of regulations for their implementation, and finally their fairly general acceptance. It was not a sharp watershed; changes were gradual, as we have seen. But young women scientists completing their education since then have had better prospects in academic careers, by and large, than their predecessors did.

Whether the climate of growing equality of opportunity has had comparable beneficial effects for older women scientists is not clear. There is anecdotal evidence that some women who for many years held research staff positions have recently achieved faculty status, and that others who were long-term instructors or lecturers have been promoted to ladder posts. The total number of such promotions cannot be very large; the entire increase of women in faculty posts between 1973 and 1977 is less than one-quarter of all women who received science doctorates from 1970 to 1977. The gains and the prospects for the older Ph.D. cohorts will need to be assessed separately from those for Ph.D.'s since 1970.

We have traced the comparative progress of women scientists since the early 1970's in some detail. In the past decade women's share of all science doctorates has doubled, from 9 percent to 18 percent, and is still increasing in all fields of science, with especially dramatic gains in the biological and social sciences and in psychology. Their qualifications match those of men: they have superior academic records upon entering graduate school, are trained in the same departments as men, complete

117

research leading to the doctorate as fast or faster than their male counterparts, and aspire to careers in teaching and research in equal proportions.

Although the unemployment rate of new women Ph.D.'s has been decreasing somewhat irregularly since 1970 (NRC, 1978) it still exceeds that of comparable male Ph.D.'s by factors as large as five. In chemistry, where women are 14 percent of new doctorates, they account for 43 percent of the unemployed Ph.D. chemists who are seeking employment, and women doctoral chemists' unemployment rate is almost equal to that for the labor force of adult women at all educational levels. While the situation is less severe in other fields, unemployment of women doctoral scientists remains high, and represents an underutilization of scientific potential as well as the material resources invested in their training. Under present and projected circumstances it is unrealistic to expect academic employment to remedy this situation. Will industry and government, where women scientists are currently severely underrepresented, absorb a larger number?

Equity in Academic Employment

Academic employment opportunities for women scientists still present a very mixed picture. Overall, a slightly larger fraction of women than men is employed in academic institutions, but there continues to be a disproportionately large number of women in two kinds of positions: part-time instructors or lecturers which are not only outside the tenure stream but also offer little chance for productive research, and postdoctoral or research staff positions which are underpaid. Spending much time in these somewhat marginal or subordinate positions may contribute substantially to cumulative disadvantage. The dependent or ancillary nature of such work probably provides little stimulus for developing the autonomy and drive necessary for a career as a teacher-scholar.

In faculty positions, women have made substantial gains as assistant professors and lesser gains in the upper ranks. The question of the real status of assistant professorships--whether these are indeed revolving doors, and whether they are more likely to be so for women than for men--remains to be resolved by further studies. A study proposed by the Commission on Human Resources to compare the career progress of men and women scientists promises to clarify the question of "revolving door" appointments and should be supported.

That the proportion of women in tenured positions continues to lag well behind that of male faculty is cause for concern. If present trends continue, it is likely that

118

there will be few tenure slots available by the time the
recently appointed women are ready to be considered for
promotion. The difficulty of making tenure decisions vis-a-
vis the growing shortage of tenure slots should not
overshadow the equal opportunity mandate. Nothing in our
findings provides a rational basis for the fact that men at
senior ranks are awarded tenure more frequently than women.
If all untenured women now at full professor ranks received
tenure overnight, the total effect on the academic economy
in the sciences would be negligible, affecting approximately
200 positions out of a total of 123,000, of which about
50,000 are men who are tenured full professors.

Although women hold a higher proportion of ladder
positions than they used to, especially at the assistant
professor level, they also hold a much larger share of off-
ladder positions than in the past. In the leading
universities women are almost half of all scientists in the
ambiguous "instructor/lecturer" category. We have no way of
knowing whether this represents a laudable effort to have
women in departments where no faculty openings exist, or a
practice of lower offers and lower promotion rates for
women.

Effectiveness of Affirmative Action

Delays in the early implementation of equal opportunity
laws cost several years during which employment of women
scientists on faculties did not change materially--years
when there was still some growth. Since 1973 growth has
been minimal in leading science departments and only
moderate in others. Employment of women faculty has
increased during these last few years, but the absolute gain
in numbers is so small as to produce only a minimal effect
on the total. Yet if it signals a trend, a change in
attitudes, it may make an important difference.

Given the long history of underutilization of women in
academe, we would not have expected material changes in the
absence of affirmative action legislation. That some
changes have occurred is probably due in part to this
legislation, although actual enforcement has been
inconsistent and scattered. The threat of possible
litigation through individual and class action suits, and of
the cost of such litigation, is probably the most effective
enforcement mechanism that exists. Even on-site compliance
reviews are apparently not being used as enforcement tools.
Undoubtedly the changes in general social climate and
growing acceptance of women in various non-traditional
professions have also contributed materially to their
growing numbers among science faculties.

With enforcement responsibility recently consolidated in the Department of Labor, some improvement in performance may result. It is hoped that more uniform administration will produce fewer capricious decisions and requests and will deal more sensitively with the resolution of difficult conflicts. We would hope to see increasing levels of cooperation on the part of both academic institutions and the federal government.

Remedial Actions

Since the total size of faculties in the research universities (and probably also in others) is unlikely to grow in the foreseeable future, we cannot expect a significant increase in the proportion of women on science faculties in the absence of special programs. Yet, when half of all undergraduates are women and graduate enrollments of women are increasing steeply, it is educationally sound and desirable to have women well represented on faculties. Otherwise we run the risk not only of losing scientific talent but of short-changing the next generation of students. If full equality of opportunity is to be attained in higher education, both male and female students will need professional women as models and mentors.

Academic Salaries

Salary equity is difficult to assess from aggregate data and is probably best studied intra-institutionally; various acceptable procedures for doing so have been published. The statistics available to us certainly suggest, at the least, that such studies are needed: some salary differences favoring men exist in all fields, at all levels, and in all categories of institutions. Whether they may be justified in individual cases on grounds of length of service or different responsibilities is not the issue. Rather, the issue is that prior conditions which determine fair salaries should not distinguish between men and women.

Advisory Committee Service

The opportunities of women scientists to augment their own horizons, profit from the personal exposure, and contribute their expertise to national science policy by serving on a variety of advisory bodies have expanded considerably in recent years.

An analysis of just where and how women advisors are being utilized--and where they are not--is hampered somewhat by the very uneven reporting practices regarding advisory committees which we have encountered. Much of our information was assembled piecemeal and is not regularly and publicly available; only NIH was able to furnish complete and full information on the composition of its committees. This is accomplished through a central office which also monitors appointments to insure adequate numbers of women.

The Issue of Mobility

The possibility that most of the manifest differences in women scientists' careers--in type of appointment, quality of institution, amount of salary, and eventual recognition-- stems from their family responsibility and their consequently reduced job mobility has been raised widely and frequently. Although most of our data do not bear on this issue directly, certain inferences are possible.

First, a clear distinction must be made between recent years, since about 1970, and the preceding period. Before the advent of affirmative action, women rarely received offers, they looked for jobs, and if they were married, usually where their husband's opportunities were best. Even the most distinguished women scientists, prospective Nobel laureates included, were not offered endowed chairs and other amenities to lure them to distant institutions. The question of independent career mobility, therefore, did not arise for them. Some achieved distinction despite the lack of offers, some did not.

More recently, career mobility has ceased to be exclusively a female problem. Young families, especially in academe, increasingly look for institutions which offer desirable opportunities to both spouses, and some leading universities have had difficulty in recruiting faculty partly because of what one characterized as the "working mate" problem (Chronicle of Higher Education, Oct. 23, 1978). Other issues, such as unwillingness to uproot children and inability to pay inflated housing costs are contributing to the problem, and professional moves are no longer regarded as quite so desirable.

To what extent such considerations have actually influenced career decisions by either women or men in the last few years is not known. It is reasonable to assume, however, 1) that single women would be free to follow career opportunities, and 2) that such mobility restrictions as may apply to married women would hold equally for all fields. The fact that single women's careers (rank, salary, etc.) resemble those of married women rather than men suggests that factors other than mobility are at work; similarly, the fact that women psychologists' academic status closely resembles men's regardless of marital status while women chemists' does not, also supports the inference that lack of mobility is a less important career factor than sex.

Nonetheless, future career mobility of both sexes would certainly be enhanced by the provision by universities of better support services in locating promising employment for a spouse. The variety of individual situations likely to be encountered does not lend itself to recommending a general program but in many cases some effort by departments, possibly through careers service offices, would be beneficial.

Recommendations

Our recommendations to the Federal Government and to academic institutions for better utilization of doctoral women scientists are as follows:

Recommendations for Fellowship and Training Programs

Recommendation 1

That federally supported scientist-teacher awards be granted annually to a minimum of 25 women for the next five years, each tenable for at least a five-year period.

These awards, based on merit, would afford a method of adding women to leading science faculties on a semi-permanent basis, increasing their numbers by about 10 percent -- a greater increase than could reasonably be accommodated by the current numbers of job openings. The more important impact would lie in the distinction of the award. The amounts of the awards would be comparable to annual faculty salaries.

It must be emphasized that we regard such awards as additions to, not substitutes for, regular faculty hiring. The cost of such a program is of course considerable, but still a good deal less than the currently ineffective efforts toward affirmative action enforcement, and the cost of litigation. Career development awards of this type have analogies in existing programs, e.g., at NIH, and are thus not a radical policy departure.

Recommendation 2

That fellowship support from federal sources be made available to enable older women scientists to update their training by means of short courses, summer work, or other specialized education.

With obsolete training and out-of-date skills, many older Ph.D.'s will have little chance to obtain highly competitive awards. Because these scientists do not exist in large homogeneous groups, it is difficult to make very detailed recommendations concerning the types of courses which should be offered or their location or sponsorship. Short courses sponsored by professional societies, such as those of the American Chemical Society, might be appropriate. Research departments and government or industrial laboratories might also be suitable places for such updating.

Recommendation 3

That an experimental program of research support and affiliation with active research departments be instituted for women scientists at teaching colleges to enhance the momentum of their research.

The prospect that this proposal offers of giving added impetus to their research by exposure to a highly active research environment and enhancing the quality of instruction in their permanent positions is considerable. Such a program could be minimal in cost, and might greatly enhance the perceptions and attitudes of research faculties toward women colleagues.

Recommendation 4

That a pilot program of awards and grants to facilitate career moves by couples be instituted on a trial basis for two to three years. Either spouse would qualify if the other partner had received a permanent appointment requiring re-location. The award would provide support for establishing a research program at a new institution.

Some leading universities have had difficulty in recruiting faculty partly because of what one characterized as the "working mate" problem (Chronicle of Higher Education, Oct. 23, 1978). This program would enhance the career mobility of scientists and afford better utilization of men and women who would otherwise face a hiatus in their research efforts.

Recommendation 5

That the National Science Foundation, as lead agency for federal research support in universities, consult with universities to devise programs that will enable non-tenure track faculty to initiate and develop independently funded research programs.

Internal regulations of most institutions do not allow or encourage off-ladder faculty to apply for independent research grants, making it difficult or impossible for such individuals to establish a research record. Women scientists are markedly overrepresented in such positions, as already noted, and their opportunities for advancement are specifically circumscribed by the limitations on grant applications.

Recommendations for Improved Monitoring of Equal Opportunity Policies

Recommendation 6

That pre-award compliance reviews give attention to promotions of women to associate or full professor ranks without tenure.

The proportion of women in senior ranks who are awarded tenure continues to lag behind that of male faculty. Nothing in our findings provides an explanation for this difference. We therefore recommend that affirmative action reporting include tenure comparisons as well as numerical gains.

Recommendation 7

That all public and private institutions be required to include academic salary information in their affirmative action reporting.

Affirmative action regulations as currently implemented in higher education rarely include regular reporting of salary data and, at least in private institutions, such information usually remains confidential. In general, salary differentials between men and women are greater in private universities than in public ones (Chronicle of Higher Education, July 17, 1978, pp. 9-12). Inclusion of salaries in reporting should encourage careful review of individual salary disparities and equalization where justified. Privacy issues need not be an insuperable obstacle; leading public research universities apparently have no problems with publication of salaries.

This recommendation is not intended to require disclosure of "supergrade" salaries for individuals of exceptional distinction, since these derive from merit considerations beyond the scope of any remedial program. The exemption would be similar to the widely accepted exemptions of certain endowed professorships from affirmative action practices.

Recommendation 8

That equal opportunity policies be linked more directly to departmental or project levels rather than to university-wide equal opportunity performance. Awards below $1 million (which do not subject the institution to a pre-award compliance review) should be contingent on satisfactory equal opportunity efforts within the department concerned, rather than requiring evidence of compliance throughout the institution.

We believe that such closer linking of awards with the units which receive the primary benefits will contribute to simplified administration, and avoid potentially penalizing entire institutions for isolated infractions.

Recommendation 9

That the National Science Foundation follow NIH in monitoring and periodically reporting on advisory committee appointments to insure that committees and panels include appropriate numbers of women scientists.

Such monitoring should also cover the various **ad** hoc panels that are frequently assembled for very specific short-term tasks. In reports that have been made available to us, **ad** hoc panels members have not always been included.

Recommendations to Institutions

Recommendation 10

That science departments and EEO officers assist in assuring that women faculty at senior ranks who are still untenured and may have been overlooked in previous reviews, are now given appropriate tenure reviews.

Recommendation 11

That departments and affirmative action officers carefully review the disproportionately high number of women appointed to off-ladder positions.

In the leading universities, women are almost half of all scientists in the ambiguous "instructor/lecturer" category. We have no way of knowing whether this represents a laudable effort to have women in departments where no faculty openings exist, or a practice of lower offers and lower promotion rates for women.

Recommendation 12

That the National Academy of Sciences/National Research Council follow the NIH in monitoring and periodically reporting on advisory committee appointments to insure that committees and panels include appropriate numbers of women scientists.

Such monitoring should also cover the various ad hoc panels that are frequently assembled for very specific short-term tasks.

Recommendation 13

That institutions give attention to facilitation of young women's scientific careers.

During periods when they are producing and raising small children many young women and men may need to interrupt or restrict their employment to part-time. Options should be available that would utilize their talents on a rigorous but less than full-time basis. Possible mechanisms would include part-time positions within the tenure track.

It is important that institutions also facilitate the development of an independent career identity. Young women today may sense pressure to become overloaded with student advising, serving on committees within the institution, and other types of university service. While these other activities are not unimportant, an over-burden may greatly restrict career development.

Conclusion

Universities as corporate entities must learn to assume a more cooperative attitude toward equal opportunity for women. Much of the cost of affirmative action is due to the adversary position taken by universities initially, and to their continuing efforts to claim a form of autonomy to which the use of public funds does not entitle them. Academic freedom does not transcend the law. It is our hope that the suggestions we have made will contribute to greater cooperation between universities and the Federal government and a lessening of the adversary climate surrounding equal opportunity problems.

REFERENCES

American Association for the Advancement of Science, Conference on Women in Scientific Research, October 17-20, 1977, Washington, D.C.

American Association of University Women, Graduate and Professional Education of Women, Washington, D.C., 1974.

Apter, Julia T., "Increasing the Professional Visiblity of Women in Academe: A Case Study," in W. Furniss and P. Graham, Eds., Women in Higher Education, American Council on Education, Washington, D.C., 1973, pp. 104-109.

Astin, Helen S., The Woman Doctorate in America, Russell Sage Foundation, New York, 1969.

Bayer, Alan E., "College and University Faculty: A Statistical Description," ACE Research Reports, 5 (5). American Council on Education, Washington, D.C., 1970.

Bayer, Alan E., and Helen S. Astin, "Sex Differentials in the Academic Reward System," Science, 188, 1975, p. 796.

Bernard, Jessie, Academic Women, Pennsylvania State University Press, University Park, 1964 (Meridian paperback 1974).

Carnegie Commission on Higher Education, Carnegie Commission Classification of Institutions of Higher Education, Carnegie Foundation for the Advancement of Teaching, Berkeley, 1973a.

Carnegie Commission on Higher Education, Opportunities for Women in Higher Education, McGraw-Hill, New York, September 1973b.

Cartter, Allan M., "Scientific Manpower for 1970-1985," Science, Vol. 172, April 9, 1971, pp. 131-140.

Centra, John A., Women, Men, and the Doctorate, Educational Testing Service, Princeton, New Jersey, September 1974.

Chronicle of Higher Education, "Faculty Compensation:
    Salaries and Fringe Benefits for Full-time Faculty
    Members at 2,500 Colleges and Universities," Vol. 26,
    Issue 19, July 17, 1978, pp. 9-12.

Cole, Jonathan R., and Stephen Cole, Social Stratification
    in Science, Chapter 5, The University of Chicago Press,
    Chicago, 1973, pp. 123-160.

Coleman, James S., The Adolescent Society, Free Press, New
    York, 1961.

Cross, K. Patricia, "The Woman Student," in W. Furniss and
    P. Graham, Eds., Women in Higher Education, American
    Council on Education, Washington, D.C., 1973, pp. 29-49.

Davies, Robert, "Expanding the Role of Women in Science,"
    Paper presented at New York Academy of Sciences
    Conference, March 1978.

Donald, M.D., S.M. Dawkins, J.L. Lovasich, E.L. Scott, M.E.
    Sherman, and J.L. Whipple, "Application of Multivariate
    Regression to Studies of Salary Differences Between Men
    and Women Faculty," Proceedings of the American
    Statistical Association, 1973, pp. 120-132.

Ernest, John, "Mathematics and Sex," The American
    Mathematical Montly, 1976.

Feldman, Saul D., Escape from the Doll's House, Carnegie
    Commission on Higher Education, McGraw-Hill, New York,
    1974.

Folger, John K., Helen S. Astin, and Alan E. Bayer, Human
    Resources in Higher Education, Russell Sage Foundation,
    New York, 1970.

Gilford, Dorothy M., and Joan Snyder, Women and Minority
    Ph.D.'s in the 1970's: A Data Book, National Academy of
    Sciences, 1977.

Gilford, Dorothy M., and Peter D. Syverson, Summary Report
    1976, Doctorate Recipients from United States
    Universities, National Academy of Sciences, March 1977.

Gilford, Dorothy M., and Peter Syverson, Summary Report
    1977, Doctorate Recipients from United States
    Universities, National Academy of Sciences, February
    1978.

Hargens, Lowell L., Jr., "The Social Context of Scientific
    Research," Ph.D. Dissertation, University of Wisconsin,
    1971.

Harmon, Lindsey R., _A Century of Doctorates_, National Academy of Sciences, Washington, D.C., 1978.

Harmon, Lindsey R., _High School Ability Patterns - A Backward Look from the Doctorate_, Scientific Manpower Report No. 6, National Academy of Sciences, Washington, D.C., August 1965.

Harris, Ann Sutherland, "The Second Sex in Academe," _AAUP Bulletin_, Vol. 56, No. 3, 1970, pp. 283-295.

Kanter, Rosabeth Moss, _Men and Women of the Corporation_, Basic Books, Inc., New York, 1977.

Keller, Evelyn Fox, "Women in Science: An Analysis of a Social Problem," _Harvard Magazine_, October 1974, pp. 14-19.

Keller, Evelyn Fox, "The Anomaly of a Woman in Physics," in _Working It Out_, Sara Ruddick and Pamela Daniels, Eds., Pantheon Books, New York, 1977.

Lester, R. A., _Antibias Regulation of Universities: Faculty Problems and Their Solution_, Part 3, Carnegie Commission on Higher Education, McGraw-Hill, New York, 1974.

Loeb, Jane W. and Marianne A. Ferber, "Representation, Performance, and Status of Women on the Faculty at the Urbana-Champaign Campus of the University of Illinois," in _Academic Women on the Move_, Alice S. Rossi and Ann Calderwood, Eds., Russel Sage Foundation, New York, 1973.

Maccoby, Eleanor E., and Carol N. Jacklin, _The Psychology of Sex Differences_, Stanford University Press, Stanford, Calif., 1974, pp. 131, 349-355, 361.

Maxfield, Betty D., Nancy C. Ahern, and Andrew W. Spisak, _Science, Engineering, and Humanities Doctorates in the United States: 1977 Profile_, National Academy of Sciences, 1978.

Maxfield, Betty D., Nancy C. Ahern, and Andrew W. Spisak, _Employment Status of Ph.D. Scientists and Engineers, 1973 and 1975_, National Academy of Sciences, Washington, D.C., 1976.

National Academy of Sciences, National Academy of Engineering, Institute of Medicine, National Research Council _Organization and Members, 1977/1978_ - National Academy of Sciences, Washington, D.C., October 1977.

National Center for Education Statistics, The Condition of Education. U.S. Government Printing Office, Washington, D.C., 1978.

National Institutes of Health, 1977 NIH Public Advisory Groups. Authority. Structure. Functions. Members. DHEW Publication No. (NIH) 77-10, July 1, 1977.

National Research Council, The Invisible University - Postdoctoral Education in the United States, National Academy of Sciences, Washington, D.C., 1969.

National Research Council, The Science Committee, A Report by the Committee on the Utilization of Young Scientists and Engineers in Advisory Services to Government, National Academy of Sciences, Washington, D.C., 1972.

National Research Council, Commission on Human Resources, Career Achievements of NDEA (Title IV) Fellows of 1959-1973, A Report to the U.S. Office of Education, National Academy of Sciences, Washington, D.C, 1977a.

National Research Council, Commission on Human Resources, Doctoral Scientists and Engineers in the United States, 1973 Profile, National Academy of Sciences, Washington, D.C., March 1974b.

National Research Council, Commission on Human Resources, Doctoral Scientists and Engineers in the United States - 1975 Profile, National Academy of Sciences, Washington, D.C., 1976a.

National Research Council, Commission on Human Resources, Personnel Needs and Training for Biomedical and Behavioral Research - 1976 Report, National Academy of Sciences, Washington, D.C., 1976b.

National Research Council, Commission on Human Resources, Personnel Needs and Training for Biomedical and Behavioral Research - 1977 Report (Volume 1 and Volume 2, appendixes), National Academy of Sciences, Washington, D.C., 1977b.

National Research Council, Commission on Human Resources, Postdoctoral Training in the Biomedical Sciences, National Academy of Sciences, Washington, D.C., December 1974c.

National Research Council, Commission on Human Resources, Research Issues in the Employment of Women: Proceedings of a Workshop, National Academy of Sciences, Washington, D.C., July 1975a.

National Research Council, Commission on Human Resources, Summary Report 1973, Doctorate Recipients from United States Universities, National Academy of Sciences, Washington, D.C., May 1974a.

National Research Council, Commission on Human Resources, Summary Report 1974, Doctorate Recipients from United States Universities, National Academy of Sciences, Washington, D.C., June 1975b.

National Research Council, Commission on Human Resources, Summary Report 1975, Doctorate Recipients from United States Universities, National Academy of Sciences, Washington, D.C., May 1976c.

National Research Council, Commission on Human Resources, Summary Report 1976, Doctorate Recipients from United States Universities, National Academy of Sciences, Washington, D.C., March 1977c.

National Research Council, Commission on Human Resources, Summary Report 1977, Doctorate Recipients from United States Universities, National Academy of Sciences, Washington, D.C., February 1978.

National Research Council, Office of Scientific Personnel, Careers of PhD's: Academic versus Nonacademic, Publ. 1577, National Academy of Sciences, Washington, D.C., 1968.

National Research Council, Office of Scientific Personnel, Employment of New Ph.D.'s and Postdoctorals in 1971, National Academy of Sciences, Washington, D.C., August 1971.

Perrucci, Carolyn, "Sex-based Professional Socialization Among Graduate Students in Science," NRC, Research Issues in the Employment of Women: Proceedings of a Workshop. National Academy of Sciences, Washington, D.C., 1975, pp. 83-123.

Rawls, Rebecca L., and Jeffrey L. Fox, "Women in Academic Chemistry Find Rise to Full Status Difficult," Chemical & Engineering News, Vol. 56, No. 37, September 11, 1978, pp. 26-36.

Reagan, Barbara B., and Betty J. Maynard, "Sex Discrimination in Universities: An Approach Through Internal Labor Market Analysis," AAUP Bulletin, Vol. 60, 1974, pp. 13-21.

Reskin, Barbara F., "Sex Differences in Status Attainment in Science: The Case of the Postdoctoral Fellowship,"

American Sociological Review, Vol. 41, August 1976, pp. 597-612.

Reskin, Barbara F., "Sex Differences in the Professional Life Chances of Chemists," Unpublished doctoral dissertation, University of Washington, Seattle, 1973.

Roose, Kenneth D., and Charles J. Andersen, *A Rating of Graduate Programs*, American Council on Education, Washington, D.C. 1970.

Rossi, Alice, and A. Calderwood, Eds., *Academic Women on the Move*, Russell Sage Foundation, New York, 1973.

Rowe, Mary P., "Behind Saturn's Rings - A Few Examples of Dust," in *Graduate and Professional Education of Women*, AMerican Association of University Women, Washington, D.C, 1974.

Sandler, Bernice and Lucy Sells, Eds., "The Hand that Rocked the Cradle has Learned to Rock the Boat," "Toward Affirmative Action," *New Directions for Institutional Research*: Jossey Bass Publishing Company, 1974.

Simon, R.J., S.M. Clark, and K. Galway, "The Women Ph.D.: A Recent Profile," in *Women and Achievement*, Martha T. Shuch Mednick, Sandra Schwartz Tangri, and Lois Wladis Hoffman, Eds., John Wiley & Sons, 1975.

Solmon, Lewis C., *Male and Female Graduate Students*, Chapter 2, Praeger Publishers, New York, 1976, p. 47.

Smith, Bruce L.R., and Joseph J. Karlesky, *The Universities in the Nation's Research Effort*, New York, 1977.

Tidball, Elizabeth Peters, "Wellesley Women in Science," *Wellesley Alumnae Magazine*, Vol. 59, 1975, pp. 1-3.

Tidball, M. Elizabeth, "Of Men and Research: The Dominant Themes in American Higher Education Include Neither Teaching Nor Women," *Journal of Higher Education*, Vol. XLVII, No. 4, July/August 1976, pp. 373-389.

Tidball, M. Elizabeth, "Perspective on Academic Women and Affirmative Action," *Educational Record*, Vol. 54, No. 2, Spring 1973, pp. 130-135.

Tidball, M. Elizabeth and Vera Kistiakowsky, "Baccalaureate Origins of American Scientists and Scholars," *Science*, Vol. 193, August 20, 1976, pp. 646-652.

Vetter, Betty M. and Eleanor L. Babco, *Professional Women and Minorities*, A Manpower Data Resource Service,

Scientific Manpower Commission, Washington, D.C., May 1975.

Weisstein, Naomi, "How Can a Little Girl Like You Teach a Great Big Class of Men?" in _Working It Out_, Sara Ruddick and Pamela Daniels, Eds., Pantheon Books, New York, 1977.

Wilsnack, Richard W., "The Uncertain Careers of Scientists in Training: The Case of Experimental Physics," paper presented at the Second Annual Meetings of the Society for the Social Studies of Science, Boston, October 1977.

APPENDIX A

AFFIRMATIVE ACTION

Federal regulations and laws require that there be no discrimination in any conditions of employment including recruitment, hiring, layoff, discharge and recall, and in-service training; opportunities for promotion; participation in training programs; wages and salaries; sick leave time and pay; vacation time and pay; overtime work and pay; medical, hospital, life and accident insurance; and optional and compulsory retirement.

Status and Orders Requiring Equal Employment Opportunity

and Affirmative Action

The Equal Pay Act of 1963, the first sex discrimination legislation enacted, requires equal pay for equal work regardless of sex. Title IX of the Education Amendments Act of 1972 extends the coverage to executive, administrative and professional employees, including all faculty; and to outside salespeople. The law is enforced by the Wage and Hour Division of the Employment Standards Administration of the Department of Labor, and reviews can be conducted without prior complaint.

If a violation is found following a review, the employer is asked to settle by raising wages and awarding back pay to underpaid workers. Should the employer refuse, the Department of Labor is authorized to go to court. No affirmative action is required other than back pay.

Executive Order 11246 as Amended by Executive Order 11375 prohibits discrimination in employment by all employers who hold federal contracts, and requires affirmative action programs by all federal contractors and subcontractors. Firms with contracts over $50,000 and 50 or more employees must develop and implement written programs of affirmative action.

The Department of Labor through its Office of Federal Contract Compliance is responsible for all policy matters under the Executive Order. However, the Department of Health, Education and Welfare does the actual review and enforces the order in universities and colleges. Failure to follow the requirements of the Executive Order can result in the delay, suspension or termination of contracts.

Title VI of the Civil Rights Act of 1964 forbids discrimination against students on the basis of race, color or national origin in all federally assisted programs. Employment is not generally covered except when employment is the purpose of the assistance. The Department of Health, Education and Welfare is the enforcement agency. Affirmative action is not required, but can be imposed after a finding of discrimination.

Title IX of the Education Amendments of 1972 forbids discrimination on the basis of sex against students and employees in all federally assisted education programs in all institutions, public and private, that receive federal monies through grants, loans or contracts. The Department of Health, Education and Welfare is the enforcement agency. Affirmative action is not required, but can be imposed after a finding of discrimination.

Title VII of the Civil Rights Act of 1964 as Amended by the Equal Employment Opportunity Act of 1972 forbids discrimination on the basis of race, color, national origin, religion or sex in any term, condition or privilege of employment by unions and by employers. The law was amended on March 24, 1972 to cover all public and private educational institutions, as well as state and local governments, and applies to all employers, public or private, whether or not they receive any federal funds. Title VII covers all private employers of 15 or more persons, and is enforced by the Equal Employment Opportunity Commission (EEOC), which is appointed by the President. Employers are required not to discriminate in employment. Title VII does not require affirmative action unless there is a finding of discrimination. The basic body of legal principles applying to employment discrimination has been developed in Title VII litigation and in cases involving the 5th and 14th amendments to the Constitution.

NOTE

1. Much of the material in this section was adapted with permission from "The Hand That Rocked the Cradle Has Learned to Rock the Boat" by Bernice Sandler from the series New Directions for Institutional Research: "Toward Affirmative Action" edited by Lucy Sells, Jossey Bass Publishing Company, 1974.

APPENDIX B

INSTITUTIONAL CLASSIFICATIONS

B-1. Ranking of Institutions
by Federal R&D Expenditures

B-2. Roose-Andersen Ratings of
Departments

137

FEDERAL OBLIGATIONS FOR RESEARCH AND DEVELOPMENT TO THE 50 UNIVERSITIES AND COLLEGES RECEIVING THE
LARGEST AMOUNTS, BY MAJOR FIELD OF SCIENCE: JULY 1, 1975 THROUGH SEPTEMBER 30, 1976

(DOLLARS IN THOUSANDS)

RANK	INSTITUTION (RANKED BY AMOUNT RECEIVED)	TOTAL	PHYSICAL SCIENCES	MATHE-MATICS	ENVIRON-MENTAL SCIENCES	ENGI-NEERING	LIFE SCIENCES	PSYCHOL-OGY	SOCIAL SCIENCES	OTHER SCIENCES, NEC
	UNITED STATES TOTAL	3,050,439	428,629	96,929	281,219	287,549	1,633,839	69,876	158,070	94,328
1	MASS INST OF TECH	92,400	26,884	3,633	11,073	25,255	18,909	791	2,692	3,163
2	STANFORD UNIV	78,033	17,713	3,686	3,897	10,552	35,191	1,388	3,875	1,731
3	UNIV OF CAL SAN DIEGO	76,249	7,386	937	35,841	3,566	25,276	523	403	2,317
4	UNIV OF WASHINGTON	74,559	5,249	1,421	13,559	7,817	40,740	884	1,803	3,086
5	UNIV OF WIS-MADISON	72,743	9,505	1,001	5,070	3,595	42,030	1,520	9,487	535
6	UNIV OF CAL LOS ANGELES	72,228	9,082	3,170	5,102	4,181	42,888	1,944	3,490	2,371
7	COLUMBIA UNIV	65,774	11,472	1,332	12,461	1,662	34,083	955	3,123	686
8	HARVARD UNIV	65,208	7,998	2,132	3,685	2,033	39,709	3,271	3,647	2,733
9	JOHNS HOPKINS UNIV	57,100	3,332	860	1,727	1,021	45,377	1,182	1,362	2,239
10	UNIV OF MINNESOTA	56,450	6,040	1,550	2,419	3,583	37,872	1,128	2,826	1,032
	TOTAL 1ST 10 INSTITUTIONS	710,744	104,661	19,722	94,834	63,265	362,075	13,586	32,708	19,893
11	UNIV OF CAL BERKELEY	54,877	10,093	2,973	5,596	6,472	24,096	1,363	3,432	852
12	UNIV OF PENNSYLVANIA	54,392	6,978	1,155	197	3,713	36,909	1,559	2,725	1,156
13	CORNELL UNIV	51,902	12,666	2,158	2,458	4,822	26,413	592	2,371	422
14	UNIV OF MICHIGAN	51,637	6,360	1,684	4,440	6,502	22,758	1,814	4,864	3,215
15	UNIV OF CHICAGO	50,948	9,577	1,583	3,101	1,223	31,803	1,034	1,790	837
16	YALE UNIV	50,415	7,144	2,422	591	1,055	35,210	1,576	1,726	691
17	UNIV OF SOUTHERN CAL	47,893	8,897	9,535	2,854	4,190	17,954	545	3,148	770
18	UNIV OF ILLINOIS-URBANA	44,570	12,791	2,919	3,037	7,032	12,833	1,082	2,087	2,789
19	NEW YORK UNIV	41,842	3,475	3,895	1,013	819	27,675	852	1,922	2,191
20	UNIV OF CAL SAN FRANCISCO	39,952	475	355	0	452	36,047	430	1,359	834
	TOTAL 1ST 20 INSTITUTIONS	1,199,172	183,117	48,401	118,121	99,545	633,773	24,433	58,132	33,650
21	PENNSYLVANIA STATE UNIV	39,363	14,576	474	2,395	5,340	13,709	296	2,165	408
22	WASHINGTON UNIV (MO)	36,931	1,926	192	648	1,679	29,981	665	551	1,289
23	DUKE UNIV	35,241	1,986	387	1,429	1,060	27,030	652	1,096	1,601
24	UNIV OF COLORADO	32,071	5,839	747	3,866	1,870	17,653	1,124	603	369
25	UNIV OF ROCHESTER	30,518	4,726	443	84	1,992	20,464	1,397	585	827
26	PURDUE UNIV	30,511	5,829	1,810	4,569	4,735	11,085	396	1,667	420
27	UNIV OF TEXAS AT AUSTIN	29,857	9,153	1,169	1,263	6,168	5,508	376	1,823	4,397
28	YESHIVA UNIV	29,734	754	141	0	152	26,224	158	1,701	604
29	UNIV OF UTAH	29,124	3,759	1,585	1,278	3,803	17,482	203	271	743
30	UNIV OF N C AT CHAP HILL	29,061	2,564	927	896	102	21,831	777	793	1,171
	TOTAL 1ST 30 INSTITUTIONS	1,521,583	234,229	56,276	134,549	126,446	824,740	30,477	69,387	45,479
31	CAL INST OF TECH	28,481	15,167	566	2,406	2,582	7,170	0	397	193
32	OHIO STATE UNIV	26,667	3,808	993	892	3,739	11,467	692	3,461	1,615
33	NORTHWESTERN UNIV	25,702	4,213	1,053	842	2,572	13,051	1,147	2,402	422
34	UNIV OF MIAMI	25,559	771	95	6,602	1,151	14,898	483	594	965
35	UNIV OF CAL DAVIS	24,742	1,482	437	943	907	19,687	82	660	544
36	COLORADO STATE UNIV	22,953	1,550	628	4,122	3,612	11,386	0	1,231	424
37	MICHIGAN STATE UNIV	22,498	3,336	368	680	1,456	12,277	327	3,981	73
38	UNIV OF PITTSBURGH	22,461	3,230	478	574	1,713	14,572	972	446	476
39	CASE WESTERN RESERVE UNIV	22,033	3,100	265	448	3,622	13,374	427	316	481
40	UNIV OF ARIZONA	21,963	5,452	327	3,890	2,401	8,687	62	884	260
	TOTAL 1ST 40 INSTITUTIONS	1,764,642	276,338	61,486	155,948	150,201	951,309	34,669	83,759	50,932
41	UNIV OF IOWA	21,760	3,026	302	184	1,158	14,645	235	1,053	1,157
42	BAYLOR COL OF MEDICINE	21,443	30	6	0	108	20,852	138	0	309
43	UNIV OF HAWAII-MANOA	21,349	3,005	398	6,324	778	7,476	151	1,350	1,867
44	J OF ALA IN BIRMINGHAM	21,139	259	453	0	0	18,975	1,182	73	197
45	UNIV OF MD COLLEGE PARK	20,485	9,934	965	2,675	2,075	3,628	264	821	123
46	PRINCETON UNIV	20,317	9,044	1,273	730	3,762	3,581	513	1,001	413
47	BOSTON UNIV	20,169	882	697	53	489	15,824	1,345	608	271
48	WOODS HOLE OCEAN INST	19,749	0	0	17,209	700	468	0	59	1,313
49	UNIV OF FLORIDA	19,569	2,963	496	1,220	2,419	11,289	494	591	97
50	CUNY MT SINAI SCH OF MED	19,560	178	0	0	86	18,860	336	0	100
	TOTAL 1ST 50 INSTITUTIONS	1,970,182	305,659	66,076	184,343	161,776	1,066,907	39,327	89,315	56,779

SEE FOOTNOTES AT END OF TABLE.

Note: Table includes data from 14 Federal agencies responsible for more than 95 percent of all Federal obligations to universities and colleges.

Source: National Science Foundation, Federal Support to Universities, Colleges, and Selected Nonprofit Institutions, Fiscal Year 1976 and Transition Quarter, NSF 77-325, 1977, p. 30.

138

ROOSE-ANDERSEN RATINGS

Unlike other classifications used in this report (AAU, Carnegie and R&D expenditures), the Roose-Andersen ratings apply to individual departments rather than to entire institutions of higher education. Also in contrast to the other categorizations which rely on one or more objective indices, these departmental rankings are based on the judgments of raters. The ratings were developed in 1969 and departments may have changed since then. Nevertheless, these ratings are applicable for the period when the most recent (1977-1978) science Ph.D.'s began their graduate training.

The following pages present the leading institutions, rated by quality of the graduate faculty, for six selected science fields:

MATHEMATICS
PHYSICS
CHEMISTRY
MICROBIOLOGY
PSYCHOLOGY
SOCIOLOGY

Source: Kenneth D. Roose and Charles J. Andersen, A Rating of Graduate Programs, American Council on Education, Washington, D.C. 1970.

Institutions Whose MATHEMATICS Departments Received Highest
Ratings (3.0 - 5.0, where 5.0 is highest), in Order of Their
Ranking, Starting with the Highest Rank.

1*	California, Berkeley
1*	Harvard
3	Princeton
4	Chicago
5	M.I.T.
6	Stanford
7	Yale
8	N.Y.U.
9	Wisconsin
10*	Columbia
10*	Michigan
12*	Cornell
12*	Illinois
14	California, Los Angeles
15*	Brandeis
15*	Brown
15*	Cal. Tech.
18*	Minnesota
18*	Pennsylvania
18*	Washington (Seattle)
21*	Purdue
21*	Rockefeller
23*	Johns Hopkins
23*	Northwestern
23*	Virginia
26*	California, San Diego
26*	Indiana

*Score and Rank are shared with another institution.

Institutions Whose PHYSICS Departments Received Highest Ratings
(3.0 - 5.0, where 5.0 is highest), in Order of Their Ranking,
Starting with the Highest Rank.

1*	California, Berkeley
1*	Cal. Tech.
1*	Harvard
4	Princeton
5*	M.I.T.
5*	Stanford
7*	Columbia
7*	Illinois
9*	Chicago
9*	Cornell
11*	California, San Diego
11*	Yale
13	Wisconsin
14*	Michigan
14*	Pennsylvania
16*	Maryland
16*	Rockefeller
18	Rochester
19	California, Los Angeles
20*	Minnesota
20*	Washington (Seattle)
22	Carnegie-Mellon
23*	Brown
23*	Duke
23*	Johns Hopkins
23*	Purdue
27*	Brandeis
27*	Colorado
27*	Iowa State (Ames)
27*	Texas

*Score and Rank are shared with another institution.

Institutions Whose CHEMISTRY Departments Received Highest Ratings
(3.0 - 5.0, where 5.0 is highest), in Order of Their Rankings,
Starting with the Highest Rank.

1	Harvard
2	Cal. Tech.
3*	California, Berkeley
3*	Stanford
5	M.I.T.
6	Illinois
7	California, Los Angeles
8*	Chicago
8*	Columbia
8*	Cornell
8*	Wisconsin
12	Yale
13	Princeton
14	Northwestern
15*	Iowa State (Ames)
15*	Purdue
17*	California, San Diego
17*	Texas
20*	Indiana
20*	Michigan
20*	Minnesota
23	Rockefeller
24*	Florida State
24*	Johns Hopkins
24*	Michigan State
24*	Penn State
24*	Rice
24*	Washington (Seattle)
30*	Brandeis
30*	Carnegie-Mellon
30*	Case Western Reserve
30*	Colorado
30*	Oregon
35*	Brown
35*	Florida
35*	Notre Dame
35*	Rochester

*Score and Rank are shared with another institution.

Institutions Whose MICROBIOLOGY Departments Received Highest
Ratings (3.0 - 5.0, where 5.0 is highest), in Order of Their
Ranking Starting with the Highest Rank.

1	Rockefeller
2*	California, Berkeley
2*	M.I.T.
4*	Cal. Tech.
4*	Harvard
4*	Illinois
7	Wisconsin
8*	Stanford
8*	Washington (Seattle)
10	Purdue
11*	California, Davis
11*	Johns Hopkins
11*	Yale
14*	Minnesota
14*	Pennsylvania
14*	Princeton
14*	Washington (St. Louis)
18*	Brandeis
18*	California, Los Angeles
18*	Case Western Reserve
18*	Chicago
18*	Indiana
18*	N.Y.U.
18*	Rutgers
25*	Columbia
25*	Duke
25*	Michigan State
25*	North Carolina
25*	Texas

*Score and Rank are shared with another institution.

Institutions Whose PSYCHOLOGY Departments Received Highest Ratings
(3.0 - 5.0, where 5.0 is highest), in Order of Their Ranking
Starting with the Highest Rank.

1	Stanford
2	Michigan
3	California, Berkeley
4	Harvard
5	Illinois
6	Pennsylvania
7*	Minnesota
7*	Wisconsin
7*	Yale
10	California, Los Angeles
11	Texas
12*	Brown
12*	M.I.T.
14*	Colorado
14*	Indiana
16*	Chicago
16*	Johns Hopkins
16*	Northwestern
16*	Penn State
20*	Cornell
20*	Iowa (Iowa City)
20*	Michigan State
20*	Rochester
24*	Duke
24*	North Carolina
24*	Oregon
27*	Columbia
27*	Princeton
27*	Washington (Seattle)
30*	Carnegie-Mellon
30*	N.Y.U.
30*	Ohio State

*Score and Rank are shared with another institution.

144

Institutions Whose SOCIOLOGY Departments Received Highest Ratings
(3.0 - 5.0, where 5.0 is highest), in Order of Their Ranking,
Starting with the Highest Rank.

1*	California, Berkeley
1*	Harvard
3	Chicago
4*	Columbia
4*	Michigan
6	Wisconsin
7	North Carolina
8	California, Los Angeles
9*	Cornell
9*	Johns Hopkins
9*	Northwestern
9*	Princeton
13*	Washington (Seattle)
13*	Yale
15*	Minnesota
15*	Stanford
17*	Michigan State
17*	Texas
19	Indiana
20*	Brandeis
20*	Pennsylvania

*Score and Rank are shared with another institution.

Appendix C

THE DOCTORATE RECORDS FILE

The Commission conducts the annual Survey of Earned Doctorates and maintains the resultant Doctorate Records File (DRF) under contract with the National Science Foundation. The Doctorate Records File contains data on earned doctorates from U.S. universities since 1920, except for professional degrees such as the M.D., D.D.S., and D.V.M.

Since 1958, the data have come from questionnaires completed each year by degree recipients at U.S. universities. The questionnaires are distributed with the cooperation of the Deans of Graduate Schools and filled in by the graduates when they complete all requirements for their doctoral degrees. The doctorate recipients provide data about their birth date and place, sex, citizenship, marital status, racial or ethnic group, educational background from high school to doctorate, sources of financial support in graduate school, and postgraduation plans. Each spring a Summary Report is published providing tabulations of these data for the doctorate recipients from U.S. universities for the prior academic year.

The File is now a computerized record of over half a million doctorate recipients from 1920 through 1977. This total includes the 31,672 records added to the File in 1977.

Because the data have been supplied by virtually all doctorates who have obtained degrees at U.S. universities since 1958, they describe the entire population. Therefore, even though the numbers in this data base are quite small for certain groups, they involve no problems of sampling error.

(1977 Questionnaire attached)

Conducted by The National Research Council in Cooperation with The American Council of Learned Societies, The Social Science Research Council, and The Graduate Deans	**Supported by** The National Science Foundation, The U.S. Office of Education, The National Endowment for the Humanities, and The National Institutes of Health

To the Doctoral Candidate:

This is a brief description of the Survey of Earned Doctorates indicating how the resulting data are used and the individual confidentiality of data is protected. The basic purpose of this Survey is to gather objective data about doctoral graduates, data that are often helpful in improving graduate education. We ask your cooperation with the project.

The information requested on the accompanying questionnaire is largely self-explanatory. Please complete it, detach it along the perforated line, and return it to your Graduate Dean. On the back of this sheet is a Specialties List with code numbers and titles for classifying your fields of specialization. This will be useful in connection with several items on the questionnaire. If none of the detailed fields listed seems to be appropriate, note the "General" and "Other" categories.

What is the Survey of Earned Doctorates?

The Survey is conducted annually by the Commission on Human Resources of the National Research Council in cooperation with the American Council of Learned Societies and the Social Science Research Council. The form is distributed with the cooperation of the Graduate Deans and filled out by all graduates who have completed requirements for their doctoral degrees. Research doctorates in all fields are included, but professional degrees such as the MD, DDS, and DVM are not included because information about recipients of those degrees is compiled elsewhere. The cumulative file goes back to 1920 and is called the Doctorate Records File.

The use of the doctoral data has been increasing, partly because of the implications for graduate education stemming from the change in the growth pattern of the number of persons receiving doctorates (562 in 1920; 3,278 in 1940; 9,735 in 1960; 29,497 in 1970; peaking at 33,727 in 1973; and now at 32,923 in 1976). This survey attempts to supply some of the information as of the time the doctorate is received.

What uses are made of the Survey data?

The data collected by this survey questionnaire become part of the Doctorate Records File maintained by the Commission on Human Resources of the National Research Council. The Survey data are collected with the intention that they will be put to use, but only under carefully defined conditions. Such data as the number of degrees awarded in each field of specialization, the educational preparation of degree recipients, their sources of financial support, the length of time required to attain the degree, and postdoctoral employment plans of doctorate recipients are of great interest to graduate schools, employers, the scholarly community, and the nation generally. The Doctorate Records File is used for a limited number of carefully defined, follow-up research studies. Each year a sample of doctorate recipients is selected for inclusion in a longitudinal research file maintained for the National Science Foundation, the National Institutes of Health, and the National Endowment for the Humanities.

Statistical summaries from the Doctorate Records File are used by educational institutions, professional societies, and government agencies. Some specific examples are:

- An extensive statistical summary of the data is published and distributed to all graduate schools about every five years.[1] These reports have been widely used by graduate schools and states to evaluate their progress in providing doctoral education. The data may also be useful to graduate students as an aid in selecting a graduate department.

- Annual reports containing statistical summaries based on the most recent year's Survey are distributed to graduate schools, government agencies, and any others on request.[2]

The confidentiality of Survey data is carefully protected.

This information is solicited under the authority of the National Science Foundation Act of 1950, as amended. All information you provide will be treated as confidential and will be used for statistical purposes only. Information will be released only in the form of statistical summaries or in a form which does not identify information about any particular person. There are only two exceptions to this policy: (1) information (name, year, and field of degree) is released to institutions from which you received degrees and to other organizations as part of the address search procedure for follow-up research studies: and (2) information from your form will be made available to the institution where you receive your doctoral degree. This latter release of information is contingent upon receipt of a signed statement from the institution that the information will be used only for internal purposes. Your response is entirely voluntary and your failure to provide some or all of the information will in no way adversely affect you.

(1) National Academy of Sciences, *Doctorate Recipients from United States Universities, 1958-1966,* Washington, D. C. 1967.
(2) National Academy of Sciences, *Summary Report 1976, Doctorate Recipients from United States Universities,* Washington, D. C. March, 1977.

NSF Form 558 1977
OMB No. 99-R0290
Approval Expires June 30, 1979

SURVEY OF EARNED, DOCTORATES

This form is to be returned to the GRADUATE DEAN, for forwarding to .... Board on Human-Resource Data and Analyses
Commission on Human Resources
National Research Council

Please print or type.

2101 Constitution Avenue, Washington, D. C. 20418

A. Name in full: .... (9-30)
                    (Last Name)   (First Name)   (Middle Name)

    Cross Reference: Maiden name or former name legally changed .... (31)

B. Permanent address through which you could always be reached: (Care of, if applicable) ....

....
          (Number)   (Street)   (City)

....
         (State)   (Zip Code)   (Or Country if not U.S.)

C. U.S. Social Security Number: __ __ __ – __ __ – __ __ __ __   (32-40)

D. Date of birth: ....   Place of birth: ....
    (41-45)   (Month)   (Day)   (Year)   (46-47)   (State)   (Or Country if not U.S.)

E. Sex: 1 ☐ Male   2 ☐ Female   (48)

F. Marital status: 1 ☐ Married   2 ☐ Not married (including widowed, divorced)   (49)

G. Citizenship: 0 ☐ U.S. native   2 ☐ Non U.S., Immigrant (Permanent Resident)
                  1 ☐ U.S. naturalized   3 ☐ Non-U.S., Non-Immigrant (Temporary Resident)   (50)
                  If Non-U.S., indicate country of present citizenship .... (51-52)

H. Racial or ethnic group: (Check all that apply.) *A person having origins in* —
    0 ☐ American Indian or Alaskan Native .....any of the original peoples of North America, and who maintain cultural identification through tribal affiliation or community recognition.
    1 ☐ Asian or Pacific Islander ....any of the original peoples of the Far East, Southeast Asia, the Indian Subcontinent, or the Pacific Islands. This area includes, for example, China, Japan, Korea, the Philippine Islands, and Samoa.
    2 ☐ Black, not of Hispanic Origin ....any of the black racial groups of Africa.
    3 ☐ White, not of Hispanic Origin ....any of the original peoples of Europe, North Africa, or the Middle East.
    4 ☐ Hispanic ....Mexican, Puerto Rican, Central or South American, or other Spanish culture or origins, regardless of race.   (53-55)

I. Number of dependents: Do not include yourself. (Dependent = someone receiving at least one half of his or her support from you) ....(56)

J. U.S. veteran status: 0 ☐ Veteran   1 ☐ On active duty   2 ☐ Non-veteran or not applicable   (57)

EDUCATION

K. High school last attended: .... (58-59)
                          (School Name)   (City)   (State)

    Year of graduation from high school: ....   (60-61)

L. List in the table below all collegiate and graduate institutions you have attended including 2-year colleges. List chronologically, and include your doctoral institution as the last entry.

Institution Name	Location	Years Attended		Major Field		Minor Field	Degree (if any)		
		From	To	Use Specialties List		Number	Title of Degree	Granted	
				Name	Number			Mo.	Yr.

M. Enter below the title of your doctoral dissertation and the most appropriate classification number and field. If a project report or a musical or literary composition (not a dissertation) is a degree requirement, please check box. ☐   (44)

    Title ....   Classify using Specialties List

    ....   Number   Name of field

    ....

N. Name the department (or interdisciplinary committee, center, institute, etc.) and school or college of the university

    which supervised your doctoral program: ....
                               (Department/Institute/Committee/Program)   (School)

O. Name of your dissertation adviser: ....
                             (Last Name)   (First Name)   (Middle Initial)

continued on next page

148

P. Please enter a "1" beside your primary source of support during graduate study. Enter a "2" beside your secondary source of support during graduate study. Check all other sources from which support was received.

58 ____ NSF Fellowship
59 ____ NSF Traineeship
60 ____ NIH Fellowship
61 ____ NIH Traineeship
62 ____ NDEA Fellowship
63 ____ Other HEW
64 ____ AEC/ERDA
      Fellowship
65 ____ NASA Traineeship

66 ____ GI Bill
67 ____ Other Federal support
      (specify) ....
68 ____ Woodrow Wilson Fellowship
69 ____ Other U.S. national fellowship

      (specify) ....
70 ____ University Fellowship
71 ____ Teaching Assistantship

72 ____ Research Assistantship
73 ____ Educational fund of
      industrial or
      business firm
74 ____ Other institutional
      funds (specify)

      ....
75 ____ Own earnings

76 ____ Spouse's earnings
77 ____ Family contribu-
      tions
78 ____ Loans (NDSL
      direct)
79 ____ Other loans
80 ____ Other (specify)

      ....

Q. Please check the space which most fully describes your status during the year immediately preceding the doctorate.

0 ☐ Held fellowship
1 ☐ Held assistantship
2 ☐ Held own research grant
3 ☐ Not employed
4 ☐ Part-time employed

Full-time
Employed in:
(Other than
0, 1, 2)

5 ☐ College or university, teaching
6 ☐ College or university, non-teaching
7 ☐ Elem. or sec. school, teaching
8 ☐ Elem. or sec. school, non-teaching
9 ☐ Industry or business
(11) ☐ Other (specify) ....
(12) ☐ Any other (specify) .... (9)

R. How many years (full-time equivalent basis) of professional work experience did you have prior to the doctorate? (include assistantships as professional experience) ....(10-11)

POSTGRADUATION PLANS

S. How well defined are your postgraduation plans?
0 ☐ Have signed contract or made definite commitment
1 ☐ Am negotiating with a specific organization, or more than one
2 ☐ Am seeking appointment but have no specific prospects

3 ☐ Other (specify) .... (12)

T. What are your immediate postgraduation plans?
0 ☐ Postdoctoral fellowship?
1 ☐ Postdoctoral research associateship?
2 ☐ Traineeship?
3 ☐ Other study (specify) ....
          Go to Item "U"
4 ☐ Employment (other than 0, 1, 2, 3)
5 ☐ Military service?
          Go to Item "V"
6 ☐ Other (specify).................... (13)

U. If you plan to be on a postdoctoral fellowship, associateship, traineeship or other study

What will be the field of your postdoctoral study?
Classify using Specialties List.
    Number   Field

.... (14-16)
What will be the primary source of support?
0 ☐ U.S. Government
1 ☐ College or university
2 ☐ Private foundation
3 ☐ Nonprofit, other than private foundation
4 ☐ Other (specify)
.... (17)
6 ☐ Unknown
      Go to Item "W"

V. If you plan to be employed, enter military service, or other —
What will be the type of employer?
0 ☐ 4-year college or university other than medical school
1 ☐ Medical school
2 ☐ Jr. or community college
3 ☐ Elem. or sec. school
4 ☐ Foreign government
5 ☐ U.S. Federal government
6 ☐ U.S. state government
7 ☐ U.S. local government
8 ☐ Nonprofit organization
9 ☐ Industry or business
(11) ☐ Self-employed
(12) ☐ Other (specify) .... (18)

Indicate _primary_ work activity with "1" in appropriate box;
secondary work activity (if any) with "2" in appropriate box.
0 ☐ Research and development
1 ☐ Teaching
2 ☐ Administration
3 ☐ Professional services to individuals
5 ☐ Other (specify).......................... (19-20)

In what field will you be working?
Please enter number from Specialties List .... (21-23)

Go to Item "W"

W. What is the name and address of the organization with which you will be associated?

....
(Name of Organization)

....
(Street)   (City, State)   (Or Country if not U.S.)   (24-29)

BACKGROUND INFORMATION

X. Please indicate, by circling the highest grade attained, the education of

your father:	none	1 2 3 4 5 6 7 8	9 10 11 12	1 2 3 4	MA, MD PhD	Postdoctoral	(30)
		Elementary school	High school	College	Graduate		
your mother:	none	1 2 3 4 5 6 7 8	9 10 11 12	1 2 3 4	MA, MD PhD	Postdoctoral	(31)
	0	1 2 3	4 5	6 7	8 9	(11)	

Signature .... Date completed ....
                                                               (32-34)

149

MATHEMATICS

000 Algebra
010 Analysis & Functional Analysis
020 Geometry
030 Logic
040 Number Theory
050 Probability & Math. Statistics (see also 544, 670, 725, 727, 920)
060 Topology
080 Computing Theory & Practice
082 Operations Research (see also 478)
085 Applied Mathematics
098 Mathematics, General
099 Mathematics, Other*

COMPUTER SCIENCES

079 Computer Sciences* (see also 437)

ASTRONOMY

101 Astonomy
102 Astrophysics

PHYSICS

110 Atomic & Molecular
120 Electromagnetism
132 Acoustics
134 Fluids
135 Plasma
136 Optics
138 Thermal
140 Elementary Particles
150 Nuclear Structure
160 Solid State
198 Physics, General
199 Physics, Other*

CHEMISTRY

200 Analytical
210 Inorganic
220 Organic
230 Nuclear
240 Physical
250 Theoretical
260 Agricultural & Food
270 Pharmaceutical
275 Polymer
298 Chemistry, General
299 Chemistry, Other*

EARTH, ENVIRONMENTAL AND MARINE SCIENCES

301 Mineralogy, Petrology
305 Geochemistry
310 Stratigraphy, Sedimentation
320 Paleontology
330 Structural Geology
341 Geophysics (Solid Earth)
350 Geomorph. & Glacial Geology
391 Applied Geol., Geol. Engr. & Econ. Geol.
395 Fuel Tech. & Petrol. Engr. (see also 479)
360 Hydrology & Water Resources
370 Oceanography
397 Marine Sciences, Other*

381 Atmospheric Physics and Chemistry
382 Atmospheric Dynamics
383 Atmospheric Sciences, Other*
388 Environmental Sciences, General (see also 480, 528)
389 Environmental Sciences, Other*
398 Earth Sciences, General
399 Earth Sciences, Other*

ENGINEERING

400 Aeronautical & Astronautical
410 Agricultural
415 Biomedical
420 Civil
430 Chemical
435 Ceramic
437 Computer
440 Electrical
445 Electronics
450 Industrial
455 Nuclear
460 Engineering Mechanics
465 Engineering Physics
470 Mechanical
475 Metallurgy & Phys. Met. Engr.
476 Systems Design & Systems Science
478 Operations Research (see also 082)
479 Fuel Tech. & Petrol. Engr. (see also 395)
480 Sanitary & Environmental
486 Mining
497 Materials Science
498 Engineering, General
499 Engineering, Other*

AGRICULTURAL SCIENCES

500 Agronomy
501 Agricultural Economics
502 Animal Husbandry
503 Food Science & Technology
504 Fish & Wildlife
505 Forestry
506 Horticulture
507 Soils & Soil Science
510 Animal Science & Animal Nutrition
511 Phytopathology
518 Agriculture, General
519 Agriculture, Other*

MEDICAL SCIENCES

522 Public Health & Epidemiology
523 Veterinary Medicine
526 Nursing
527 Parasitology
528 Environmental Health
534 Pathology
536 Pharmacology
537 Pharmacy
538 Medical Sciences, General
539 Medical Sciences, Other*

BIOLOGICAL SCIENCES

540 Biochemistry

542 Biophysics
544 Biometrics & Biostatistics (see also 050, 670, 725, 727, 920)
545 Anatomy
546 Cytology
547 Embryology
548 Immunology
550 Botany
560 Ecology
562 Hydrobiology
564 Microbiology & Bacteriology
566 Physiology, Animal
567 Physiology, Plant
569 Zoology
570 Genetics
571 Entomology
572 Molecular Biology
576 Nutrition and/or Dietetics
578 Biological Sciences, General
579 Biological Sciences, Other*

PSYCHOLOGY

600 Clinical
610 Counseling & Guidance
620 Developmental & Gerontological
630 Educational
635 School Psychology
641 Experimental
642 Comparative
643 Physiological
650 Industrial & Personnel
660 Personality
670 Psychometrics (see also 050, 544, 725, 727, 920)
680 Social
698 Psychology, General
699 Psychology, Other*

SOCIAL SCIENCES

700 Anthropology
708 Communications*
710 Sociology
720 Economics (see also 501)
725 Econometrics (see also 050, 544, 670, 727, 920)
727 Statistics (see also 050, 544, 670, 725, 920)
740 Geography
745 Area Studies*
751 Political Science
752 Public Administration
755 International Relations
770 Urban & Reg. Planning
798 Social Sciences, General
799 Social Sciences, Other*

HUMANITIES

802 History & Criticism of Art
804 History, American
805 History, European
806 History, Other*
807 History & Philosophy of Science
808 American Studies
809 Theatre and Theatre Criticism
830 Music
831 Speech as a Dramatic Art (see also 885)

832 Archeology
833 Religion (see also 881)
834 Philosophy
835 Linguistics
836 Comparative Literature
878 Humanities, General
879 Humanities, Other*

LANGUAGES & LITERATURE

811 American
812 English
821 German
822 Russian
823 French
824 Spanish & Portuguese
826 Italian
827 Classical*
829 Other Languages*

EDUCATION

900 Foundations: Social & Philosoph.
910 Educational Psychology
908 Elementary Educ., General
909 Secondary Educ., General
918 Higher Education
919 Adult Educ. & Extension Educ.
920 Educ. Meas. & Stat.
929 Curriculum & Instruction
930 Educ. Admin. & Superv.
940 Guid., Couns., & Student Pers.
950 Special Education (Gifted, Handicapped, etc.)
960 Audio-Visual Media

TEACHING FIELDS

970 Agriculture Educ.
972 Art Educ.
974 Business Educ.
976 English Educ.
978 Foreign Languages Educ.
980 Home Economics Educ.
982 Industrial Arts Educ.
984 Mathematics Educ.
986 Music Educ.
988 Phys. Ed., Health, & Recreation
989 Reading Education
990 Science Educ.
992 Social Science Educ.
993 Speech Education
994 Vocational Educ.
996 Other Teaching Fields*

998 Education, General
999 Education, Other*

OTHER PROFESSIONAL FIELDS

881 Theology (see also 833)
882 Business Administration
883 Home Economics
884 Journalism
885 Speech & Hearing Sciences (see also 831)
886 Law & Jurisprudence
887 Social Work
891 Library & Archival Science
897 Professional Field, Other*

899 OTHER FIELDS*

* Identify the specific field in the space provided on the questionnaire.

THE COMPREHENSIVE ROSTER AND SURVEY OF DOCTORATE RECIPIENTS

The Comprehensive Roster of Doctorate Recipients, compiled by the National Research Council's Commission on Human Resources, contains data on 402,000 individuals. The roster consists of scientists and engineers who earned Ph.D.'s within the period 1934-1976 (including recipients of degrees from foreign universities who were employed as scientists and engineers in the United States), and humanists who earned doctorates from U.S. universities within the period 1930-1976. The roster was compiled primarily from the NRC's Doctorate Records File and the NSF's National Register of Scientific and Technical Personnel. Also consulted were American Men and Women of Science, college and university catalogues, and other sources.

Surveys of a sample of the doctorate recipients were conducted in 1973, 1975, and 1977 to collect longitudinal data on field, type of employer, salary, and other employment information. The 1977 survey, which was the first to include Ph.D.'s in the humanities, included a sample of 79,400 individuals of which 65,100 were scientists and engineers.

The sample was stratified by field of doctorate or field of science/engineering employment, the year the doctorate was awarded, degree category (i.e., U.S. doctorates in science, engineering, or the humanities; U.S. doctorates in education or professional fields working in science or engineering; and doctorates from foreign institutions who were employed as scientists or engineers), sex, and race/ethnic group. A sampling rate was set for each stratum, varying from 7 to 100 percent, in order to provide sufficiently large samples for certain subgroups of the population, e.g., women. Within each stratum a simple random sample was selected. Responses from 50,600 Ph.D.'s or 64 percent of the sample, were weighted to estimate the U.S. doctoral population.

The questionnaire used in 1977 is reproduced on the following pages. Details of the survey, sampling frame, response rates, weighting procedure, and sampling errors may be found on pp. 2-5 and in Appendices A-E of the report, Science, Engineering, and Humanities Doctorates in the United States, 1977 Profile.

The Comprehensive Roster and Survey was initiated by the National Science Foundation and is currently supported by the Foundation, the National Institutes of Health, and the National Endowment for the Humanities.

1977 SURVEY OF DOCTORATE RECIPIENTS

OMB No. 099-RO294

CONDUCTED BY THE NATIONAL RESEARCH COUNCIL WITH THE SUPPORT OF THE NATIONAL SCIENCE FOUNDATION, THE NATIONAL ENDOWMENT FOR THE HUMANITIES, AND THE NATIONAL INSTITUTES OF HEALTH

THE ACCOMPANYING LETTER requests your assistance in this biennial survey of Ph.D.'s in the humanities, sciences, and engineering.

PLEASE READ the instructions for each question carefully and answer by printing your reply or checking the appropriate box.

PLEASE CHECK the pre-printed information to be certain that it is correct and complete.

PLEASE RETURN the completed form in the enclosed envelope to the Commission on Human Resources, JH 638, National Research Council, 2101 Constitution Avenue, N.W., Washington, D.C. 20418.

NOTE: THIS INFORMATION IS SOLICITED UNDER THE AUTHORITY OF THE NATIONAL SCIENCE FOUNDATION ACT OF 1950, AS AMENDED. ALL INFORMATION YOU PROVIDE WILL BE TREATED AS CONFIDENTIAL AND USED FOR STATISTICAL PURPOSES ONLY. INFORMATION WILL BE RELEASED ONLY IN THE FORM OF STATISTICAL SUMMARIES OR IN A FORM WHICH DOES NOT IDENTIFY INFORMATION ABOUT ANY PARTICULAR PERSON. YOUR RESPONSE IS ENTIRELY VOLUNTARY AND YOUR FAILURE TO PROVIDE SOME OR ALL OF THE REQUESTED INFORMATION WILL IN NO WAY ADVERSELY AFFECT YOU.

_____

_____

_____

If your name and address are incorrect, please enter correct information above. Include ZIP CODE.

If there is an alternate address through which you can always be reached, please provide it on the line below. (10)

C/O	Number Street	City	State	ZIP Code (11)

1. Date of Birth Mo. Day Year (12-16)	2. State or Foreign Country of Birth (17-18)	3. Citizenship 0 ☐ U.S.A. 1 ☐ Non-U.S.A., Specify Country _____ (20-21) (19)	4. Sex 1 ☐ M 2 ☐ F (22)

5. What is your racial background?
- 0 ☐ American Indian or Alaskan Native
- 1 ☐ Asian or Pacific Islander
- 2 ☐ Black
- 3 ☐ White

(23)

5a. Is your ethnic heritage Hispanic?
- 0 ☐ Yes
- 1 ☐ No

(24)

6. List in the table below all collegiate and graduate degrees, excluding honorary degrees, that have been awarded to you. Please check the pre-printed information, including the number and name of the specialty from the list on page 4, to be certain that it is correct and complete.

Type of Degree	Granted Mo. Yr.	Major Field (Use Specialties List) Name Number	Institution Name	City (or Campus) & State
Bachelor's				
Master's				
Doctorate				
Other (Specify) _____				

7. What was your employment status as of February 6-12, 1977? (Check only one category.)

Employed full-time in field of Ph.D. .... ☐ 1
Employed full-time in field other than field of Ph.D. .... ☐ 2
Employed part-time .... ☐ 3
   Were you seeking full-time employment?
     1 ☐ Yes   2 ☐ No   (66)
Postdoctoral appointment (fellowship, traineeship, research associateship, etc.) .... ☐ 4
Unemployed and seeking employment .... ☐ 5
Not employed and not seeking employment .... ☐ 6
Retired and not employed .... ☐ 7
Other, specify: _____ ☐ 8

(65)

→ 7a. If you were employed full-time during February 6-12, 1977, in a field other than your field of Ph.D., what was the MOST important reason for taking the position?

Preferred position outside Ph.D. field .... ☐ 1
Promoted out of position in Ph.D. field .... ☐ 2
Better pay .... ☐ 3
Locational factors .... ☐ 4
Position in Ph.D. field not available .... ☐ 5

Other, specify: _____ ☐ 6

(67)

If you checked 5, 6 or 7, ANSWER ONLY 8a, 9a, 13, 14 and 17 of the following questions.

152

8. Which category below best describes the type of organization of your principal employment OR postdoctoral appointment during February 6-12, 1977? (Check only one category.)

Business or industry .... ☐ 1
Junior college, 2-year college, technical institute .... ☐ 2
Medical school... ☐ 3
4-Year college... ☐ 4
University, other than medical school .... ☐ 5
Elementary or secondary school system .... ☐ 6
Private foundation... ☐ 7
Museum or historical society .... ☐ 8
Research library or archives .... ☐ 9

Hospital or clinic.. ☐ 10
U.S. military service, active duty, or Commissioned Corps,
   e.g., USPHS, NOAA .... ☐ 11
U.S. government, civilian employee............................... ☐ 12
State government.. ☐ 13
Local or other government, specify:

_____ ☐ 14
Non-profit organization, other than those listed above.............. ☐ 15

Other, specify: _____ ☐ 16
(68-69)

8a. Which of the above categories best describes the type of organization related to your first position following the receipt of your doctorate? (List only one category)

_____
Type of Organization   (70-71)

9. What percent of time did you devote to each of the following activities during the week of February 6-12, 1977? (Total should equal 100%)
What were your primary (A) and secondary (B) work activities? (Check only one in each column.)

	%	A	B
Management or administration of			
Research and development	_____ (10)	☐ 1	☐
Other than research and development	_____ (12)	☐ 2	☐
Both	_____ (14)	☐ 3	☐
Basic research	_____ (16)	☐ 4	☐
Applied research	_____ (18)	☐ 5	☐
Development of equipment, products, systems, data	_____ (20)	☐ 6	☐
Development of humanities resource materials	_____ (22)	☐ 7	☐
Design	_____ (24)	☐ 8	☐
Teaching	_____ (26)	☐ 9	☐
Writing, editing	_____ (28)	☐ 10	☐
Curatorial	_____ (30)	☐ 11	☐
Production	_____ (32)	☐ 12	☐
Consulting, specify: _____	_____ (34)	☐ 13	☐
Professional services to individuals	_____ (36)	☐ 14	☐
Quality control, inspection, testing	_____ (38)	☐ 15	☐
Sales, marketing, purchasing, estimating	_____ (40)	☐ 16	☐
Other, specify: _____	_____ (42)	☐ 17	☐
	Total = 100%	(44-47)	

9a. Which of the above categories best describes the primary work activity related to your first position following the receipt of your doctorate?

_____
Primary Work Activity   Number   (48-49)

10. From the Degree and Employment Specialties List on page 4 select and enter both the number and title of the employment specialty most closely related to your principal employment or postdoctoral appointment during the week of February 6-12, 1977. Write in your specialty if it is not on the list.

_____
Number   Title of Employment Specialty   (50-52)

11. Please give the name of your principal employer (organization, company, etc. or, if self employed, write "self"), and actual place of employment as of the week of February 6-12, 1977.

_____
Name of Employer   (53-58)

_____
Number   Street

_____
City   State   ZIP Code
                            (59-63)

12. What was the basic annual salary* associated with your principal professional employment during the week of February 6-12, 1977? If you were on a postdoctoral appointment (e.g., fellowship, traineeship, research associateship), what was your annual stipend plus allowances?

$ _____ per year   (64-66)

*NOTE: Basic annual salary is your annual salary before deductions for income tax, social security, retirement, etc., but does not include bonuses, overtime, summer teaching, or other payment for professional work.

IF ACADEMICALLY EMPLOYED:

a. Check whether salary was for ☐ 9-10 months or ☐ 11-12 months. (67)

b. Did you hold a tenured position during February 6-12, 1977?   0 ☐ Yes   1 ☐ No (68)
        If Yes, what year was tenure granted? _____   (69-70)

c. What was the rank of your position? (Check only one.)
1 ☐ Professor   4 ☐ Instructor
2 ☐ Associate Professor   5 ☐ Lecturer
3 ☐ Assistant professor   6 ☐ Other, specify: _____
                                    (71)

d. What, if any, administrative position did you hold?
1 ☐ Dean   4 ☐ Vice-President or Vice-Chancellor
2 ☐ Department Chairman   5 ☐ Other, specify: _____
3 ☐ President or Chancellor   6 ☐ Does not apply
                                      (72)

153

13. How many full-time equivalent years of professional work experience, including teaching, have you had? _____ Year(s)

(73-74)

14. Following completion of your doctorate have you ever held a fellowship, traineeship, or research associateship? 0 ☐ Yes   1 ☐ No

(75)

15. Listed below are selected topics of national interest. If you devoted a proportion of your professional time which you considered significant to any of these problem areas during the week of February 6-12, 1977, please check the box for the one on which you spent the MOST time.

1 ☐ Health
2 ☐ Defense
3 ☐ Environmental protection, pollution control
4 ☐ Education
5 ☐ Space

6 ☐ Crime prevention and control
7 ☐ Energy and fuel
8 ☐ Food and other agricultural products
9 ☐ Natural resources,other than fuel or food
10 ☐ Community development and services

11 ☐ Housing (planning, design, construction)
12 ☐ Transportation, communications
13 ☐ Cultural life
14 ☐ Other area, specify: _____
15 ☐ Does not apply

(10-11)

16. Was any of your work in the week of February 6-12, 1977 supported or sponsored by U.S. Government funds?

0 ☐ Yes   1 ☐ No   2 ☐ Don't know   (12)

If Yes, which of the following federal agencies or departments were supporting the work? (Check all that apply.)

13 ☐ Agency for International Development
14 ☐ Energy Research & Development Administration
15 ☐ Environmental Protection Agency
16 ☐ National Aeronautics & Space Administration
17 ☐ National Endowment for the Arts
18 ☐ National Endowment for the Humanities
19 ☐ National Science Foundation
20 ☐ Nuclear Regulatory Commission
21 ☐ Smithsonian Institution
22 ☐ Department of Agriculture
23 ☐ Department of Commerce
24 ☐ Department of Defense

Department of Health. Education, and Welfare
25 ☐ National Institutes of Health
26 ☐ Alcohol, Drug Abuse & Mental Health Administration
27 ☐ National Institute of Education
28 ☐ Office of Education
29 ☐ Other, specify: _____
30 ☐ Department of Housing and Urban Development
31 ☐ Department of the Interior
32 ☐ Department of Justice
33 ☐ Department of Labor
34 ☐ Department of State
35 ☐ Department of Transportation
36 ☐ Other agency or department, specify: _____
37 ☐ Don't know source agency

17. If you received your doctoral degree in science or engineering or are employed as a scientist or engineer, please check all that apply below:

☐ (a) Changed positions during the period 1973 to 1976.
☐ (b) Received doctoral degree in 1965 or later and employed sometime since receiving your doctoral degree in industry, government, or as non-faculty academic staff.
☐ (c) Held a postdoctoral appointment any year during 1970-1976 inclusive.
☐ (d) None of the above apply.   (38-41)

If you have checked a, b, or c, please give a brief career history starting with the position prior to your present position and continuing back in time for a maximum of four positions after receiving your doctoral degree (Include postdoctoral appointments).

Name and Location (City and State) of Employer	Position Title	Dates Held	Primary Work Activity*	Employment Specialty (Use Degree & Employ-ment Specialties List)	Reason for Leaving Position
1.					
2.					
3.					
4.					

*Enter code (1-17) from the list given in item 9.

(a) Of the positions described above, as well as your present position, please check any in which your doctoral training was/is not being used.

☐ Position 1   ☐ Position 2   ☐ Position 3   ☐ Position 4   ☐ Present Position   ☐ None

(74-79)

154

DEGREE AND EMPLOYMENT SPECIALTIES LIST

MATHEMATICAL SCIENCES

000 - Algebra
010 - Analysis & Functional Analysis
020 - Geometry
030 - Logic
040 - Number Theory
052 - Probability
055 - Math. Statistics (see also 544, 670, 725, 729)
060 - Topology
082 - Operations Research (see also 478)
085 - Applied Mathematics
089 - Combinatorics & Finite Mathematics
091 - Physical Mathematics
098 - Mathematics, General
099 - Mathematics, Other*

COMPUTER SCIENCES

071 - Theory
072 - Software Systems
073 - Hardware Systems
074 - Intelligent Systems
079 - Computer Sciences, Other

PHYSICS & ASTRONOMY

101 - Astronomy
102 - Astrophysics
110 - Atomic & Molecular Physics
120 - Electromagnetism
130 - Mechanics
132 - Acoustics
134 - Fluids
135 - Plasma Physics
136 - Optics
138 - Thermal Physics
140 - Elementary Particles
150 - Nuclear Structure
160 - Solid State
198 - Physics, General
199 - Physics, Other*

CHEMISTRY

200 - Analytical
210 - Inorganic
215 - Synthetic Inorganic & Organometallic
220 - Organic
225 - Synthetic Organic & Natural Products
230 - Nuclear
240 - Physical
245 - Quantum
250 - Theoretical
255 - Structural
260 - Agricultural & Food
265 - Thermodynamics & Material Properties
270 - Pharmaceutical
275 - Polymers
280 - Biochemistry (see also 540)
285 - Chemical Dynamics
298 - Chemistry, General
299 - Chemistry, Other*

EARTH, ENVIRONMENTAL AND MARINE SCIENCES

301 - Mineralogy, Petrology
305 - Geochemistry
310 - Stratigraphy, Sedimentation
320 - Paleontology
330 - Structural Geology
341 - Geophysics (Solid Earth)
350 - Geomorph. & Glacial Geology
391 - Applied Geol., Geol. Engr. & Econ. Geol.
395 - Fuel Tech. & Petrol. Engr. (see also 479)
360 - Hydrology & Water Resources
370 - Oceanography
397 - Marine Sciences, Other*
381 - Atmospheric Physics & Chemistry
382 - Atmospheric Dynamics
383 - Atmospheric Sciences, Other*
388 - Environmental Sciences, General (see also 480, 528)
389 - Environmental Sciences, Other*
398 - Earth Sciences, General
399 - Earth Sciences, Other*

ENGINEERING

400 - Aeronautical & Astronautical
410 - Agricultural
415 - Biomedical
420 - Civil
430 - Chemical
435 - Ceramic
440 - Electrical
445 - Electronics
450 - Industrial & Manufacturing
455 - Nuclear
460 - Engineering Mechanics
465 - Engineering Physics
470 - Mechanical
475 - Metallurgy & Phys. Met. Engr.
476 - Systems Design & Systems Science (see also 072, 073, 074)
478 - Operations Research (see also 082)
479 - Fuel Technology & Petrol. Engr.
480 - Sanitary & Environmental
486 - Mining
497 - Materials Science Engr.
498 - Engineering, General
499 - Engineering, Other*

AGRICULTURAL SCIENCES

500 - Agronomy
501 - Agricultural Economics
502 - Animal Husbandry
504 - Fish & Wildlife
505 - Forestry
506 - Horticulture
507 - Soils & Soil Science
510 - Animal Science & Animal Nutrition
511 - Phytopathology
517 - Food Science & Technology (see also 573)
518 - Agriculture, General
519 - Agriculture, Other*

MEDICAL SCIENCES

520 - Medicine & Surgery
522 - Public Health & Epidemiology
523 - Veterinary Medicine
524 - Hospital Administration
526 - Nursing
527 - Parasitology
528 - Environmental Health
534 - Pathology
536 - Pharmacology
537 - Pharmacy
538 - Medical Sciences, General
539 - Medical Sciences, Other*

BIOLOGICAL SCIENCES

540 - Biochemistry (see also 280)
542 - Biophysics
543 - Biomathematics
544 - Biometrics, Biostatistics (see also 055, 670, 725, 729)
545 - Anatomy
546 - Cytology
547 - Embryology
548 - Immunology
550 - Botany
560 - Ecology
562 - Hydrobiology
564 - Microbiology & Bacteriology
566 - Physiology, Animal
567 - Physiology, Plant
569 - Zoology
570 - Genetics
571 - Entomology
572 - Molecular Biology
573 - Food Science & Technology (see also 517)
574 - Behavior/Ethology
576 - Nutrition & Dietetics
578 - Biological Sciences, General
579 - Biological Sciences, Other*

PSYCHOLOGY

600 - Clinical
610 - Counseling & Guidance
620 - Developmental & Gerontological
630 - Education
635 - School Psychology
641 - Experimental
642 - Comparative
643 - Physiological
650 - Industrial & Personnel
660 - Personality
670 - Psychometrics (see also 055, 544, 725, 729)
680 - Social
698 - Psychology, General
699 - Psychology, Other*

SOCIAL SCIENCES

700 - Anthropology
703 - Archeology
708 - Communications*
709 - Linguistics
710 - Sociology
720 - Economics (see also 501)
725 - Econometrics (see also 055, 544, 670, 729)
729 - Social Statistics (see also 055, 544, 670, 725)
740 - Geography
745 - Area Studies*
751 - Political Science
752 - Public Administration
755 - International Relations
770 - Urban & Regional Planning
775 - History & Philosophy of Science
798 - Social Sciences, General
799 - Social Sciences, Other*

HUMANITIES

802 - History & Criticism of Art
804 - History, American
805 - History, European
806 - History, Other*
808 - American Studies
830 - Music
831 - Speech as a Dramatic Art (see also 885)
833 - Religion (see also 881)
834 - Philosophy
836 - Comparative Literature
878 - Humanities, General
879 - Humanities, Other*
891 - Library & Archival Sciences

LANGUAGES & LITERATURE

811 - American
812 - English
821 - German
822 - Russian
823 - French
824 - Spanish & Portuguese
826 - Italian
827 - Classical*
829 - Other Languages*

EDUCATION & OTHER PROFESSIONAL FIELDS

938 - Education
801 - Art, Applied
881 - Theology (see also 833)
882 - Business Administration
883 - Home Economics
884 - Journalism
885 - Speech & Hearing Sciences (see also 831)
886 - Law, Jurisprudence
887 - Social Work
897 - Professional Field, Other*

899 - OTHER FIELDS*

*Identify the specific field in the space on the questionnaire.